THE ART OF
TRAVEL AND TOURISM

Edited by

Dr. Vinod A. S.

Infinity
Indica
Publishers

Imprint of
Infinity Indica OPC Private Limited
Trivandrum, Kerala, India
Contact@infinityindica.in

The moral right of the editor has been asserted.

Printed at: Akshara Offset Trivandrum

Layout by Infinity Indica Publishers

Cover by Adithya Sankar

ISBN: 978-93-91700-38-6

First Edition September 2022

www.infinityindica.in

Price: ₹ 350/-

THE ART OF TRAVEL AND TOURISM

CHIEF EDITOR

Dr. Vinod A. S.

Assistant Professor
Post Graduate and Research Department Of Commerce
Mahatma Gandhi College Thiruvananthapuram,Kerala,India
Affiliated To University Of Kerala

PREFACE

The book titled "THE ART OF TRAVEL AND TOURISM" contains the chapters related to travel and tourism and its related areas . The chapters include the contributions of experts at their academic field. I am thankful to the contributors for their academic contents in edited book titled THE ART OF TRAVEL AND TOURISM. I express my love and affection to my parents, wife, kids, colleagues and friends to makes my dream come true.

Dr. Vinod A. S.
Chief Editor

CONTENTS

Richu Mathew,
Research Scholar,
CMS College Kottayam

Clement Mathew Kuriakose,
Research Scholar,
CMS College Kottayam

Dr. Mathew Jacob
Research Supervisor,
Mahatma Gandhi University Kottayam

Lt. Seena V.
Assistant Professor of Economics
TKMM College Nangiarkulangara

Dr. Sheela M.C.
Associate Professor of Economics & Research Guide
University College Thiruvananthapuram

Minu Rose Francis
Assistant Professor,
Amal Jothi College of Engineering,
Koovappally

Dr Reshmi R. Prasad,
Principal, All Saints' College,
Trivandrum

Dr. Reji Vargheese Mekkaden,
Associate Professor, Department of Political Science,
St. George's College Aruvithura, Kottayam

Dr. Raji Mohan
Assistant Professor
PG Department of Commerce and Research Centre
St. Xavier's College for Women, Aluva

Remya Hari
Research Scholar
PG Department of Commerce and Research Centre
St. Xavier's College for Women, Aluva

Mishel Elizabeth Jacob
Research Scholar,
School of Management and Business Studies,
Mahatma Gandhi University
Kottayam

Ms. Jisny K.E,
Post Graduate student,

Department of Home Science
St. Teresa's College, Kerala, India

Smt Teresa Kuncheria
Associate Professor,
Department of Home Science
St. Teresa's College, Kerala, India

Sumi John
Research Scholar, Department of Commerce
University of Kerala

Ms. Jeena Joy
Research Scholar,
Mahatma Gandhi University Kottayam

Misha V,
Assistant Professor of Commerce,
Sree Narayana College, Kollam

Andrea Varghese
Adhoc Faculty,
St Josephs College (Autonomous),
Irinjalakuda

Remya S.
Assistant Professor,
St Josephs College (Autonomous),
Irinjalakuda

CHAPTER 1

EXPERIENTIAL TOURISM – A MEANS TO ENHANCE BRAND EXPERIENCE OF KERALA AS A TOURIST DESTINATION

Richu Mathew,
Research Scholar,
CMS College Kottayam

Clement Mathew Kuriakose,
Research Scholar,
CMS College Kottayam

Dr. Mathew Jacob
Research Supervisor,
Mahatma Gandhi University Kottayam

ABSTRACT

Kerala model tourism has been a very successful destination brand worldwide. Kerala began marketing its tourist destinations under the tagline "God's Own Country" by the end of the twentieth century, attracting numerous visitors from India and abroad. Although the earlier scenario wherein mass tourism had a good scope of being marketed, nowadays, people tend to demand more authentic, personal and real-life experiences from tourist destinations. In this regard, experiential tourism has proven to be highly effective in attracting potential visitors to destinations. The present chapter discusses various aspects relating to destination brand experience, the scope of Kerala to provide varied experiences, experiential tourism and some recent initiatives of Kerala in this regard.

Keywords: Destination Brand Experience, Experiential tourism, STREET project

Tourism is "a social, cultural and economic phenomenon which entails the movement of people to countries or places outside their usual environment for personal or business/professional purposes", according to UNWTO. Tourism is one of the primary revenue sources for many places and nations. In the case of Kerala also, tourism is one of the major sectors that the Government focuses on earning a good amount of revenue and help increase employment opportunities for the residents of such places.

As people move 'outside their usual environment' to other places, such places should provide unique experiences for such visitors, prompting them to revisit such destinations in the future. Kerala is rich in its culture and natural beauty, and it is capable of providing unique experiences to visitors. Kerala has been a very successful destination brand for many years in the tourism industry. The success of Kerala marketing lies in the fact that it was able to project its multi-dimensional experiences to the world, thereby attracting tourists from other states of India and various parts of the world.

The present chapter discusses Kerala as a destination brand, Kerala's ability to enhance destination brand experience and experiential tourism.

DESTINATION BRANDING

Cai (2002) defines a destination brand as "perceptions about a place as reflected by the associations held in tourist memory". Destination branding is about identifying the destination's most vital and most competitively appealing assets in the eyes of its prospective visitors, building a story from these that makes the destination unique from its competitors, and running this narrative consistently through all marketing communications.

Destination branding means branding of places or destinations. In general, tourist locations or regions are subject to destination branding. As in the case of branding of products or services, destination branding also has its core in Intellectual Property Rights with the registration of logos or taglines that are closely associated with a place. However, destination branding is multi-dimensional compared to product or service branding. Places are permanently anchored into history, culture or ecosystem that marks the speciality or unique offering of the place. Thus, a product or service brand is related to something flexible according to customer needs, while a destination brand is associated with something already in existence.

Destination branding is critical, particularly in the present era. Branding tourist destinations is an essential strategy that helps marketers distinguish one destination from competing destinations. For example, there are numerous tourist spots to visit in India. A potential visitor to choose one particular place depends upon the strength of the marketing efforts of the place. Through destination branding, marketers try to invoke positive feelings and imaginativeness regarding a place in people's minds. This has a significant impact on the choice of people.

DESTINATION BRAND EXPERIENCE

Destination Brand Experience is a fundamental concept related to destination branding. Brakus et al. (2009) identified that existing brand experience literature focuses more on product utilitarian experiences than brand. They identified five critical areas of experience, stating "the feel experience includes moods and emotions. The think experience includes convergent/analytical and divergent/imaginative thinking. The act experience refers to motor actions and behavioral experiences. Finally, the relate experience refers to social experiences" (p. 54).

Brakus et al. (2009) suggested the final scale consisting of four aspects: sensory, affective, intellectual, and behavioural experiences. Sensory experiences are based on visual or other sensory impacts, affective experiences induce emotions or feelings, behavioural experiences are related to activities, and bodily experiences and intellectual experiences invokes thoughts and curiosity. Although the scale mentioned above was not developed in a tourism context, Barnes et al. (2014) adopted the same scale for measuring the destination brand experience of three locations. Barnes et al. (2014) identified positive relation among destination brand experience, tourist satisfaction, intention to recommend and intention to revisit. However, only sensory and affective aspects of brand experiences showed a positive relationship with the above aspects in the study.

KERALA AS A DESTINATION BRAND

Brand Kerala is one of the most tourism success stories in India. Kerala has been marketing its tourism initiatives under the tagline "God's Own Country" since the early 1990s. The tagline was coined by Walter Mendez and his team at Mudra Communications. Kerala was relatively an unknown tourism destination in India till the early 1980s. The marketing campaigns by the Kerala Tourism Development Corporation (KTDC) gave a boost to Kerala as a tourist destination. The marketers successfully projected Kerala as a must-visit spot in the global arena by marketing every aspect of Kerala from towns, museums, culture, village experiences, hill stations and beaches.

As far as marketing is concerned, the projection of various distinct experiences is critical as it impacts the expectations of potential tourists while selecting a tourist location. Today, where visitors are looking forward to more authentic and real-life experiences, the projection and creation of such an image is of higher significance. As discussed above, brand experiences have many dimensions, and multiple experiences will help enhance the overall brand experience of visitors. Inculcating experiential tourism and brand experience in Kerala will be highly useful in this regard, especially in the post-covid stage wherein the tourism industry is in its recovery period. Building strong brand experiences will enhance the capability of Kerala as a destination brand to attract more visitors to it.

EXPERIENTIAL TOURISM

Experience and travel are acknowledged as education by themselves. Integrating both will have the synergy effect in enriching life and hence be domestic tourists or international tourists now attracted towards experiential tourism. Experiential tourism is the form of tourism in which tourists are provided with the chance to experience the country, city, village, or a particular place by actively and meaningfully engaging with its history, people, culture, food, and environment. It includes the people interacted, the sites visited, the activities participated in, and peak; the memories created. There is the active involvement of tourists in various engagements under experiential tourism. The immersive experience offered to experiential travellers helps them better understand the environment of the place they visited, be it's heritage, culture, history, or anything. In the words of (Rajan, 2015), experiential tourism is creating experiences that engage visitors in a series of memorable activities, revealed over a period of time, that are inherently personal, engage the senses, and make connections on an emotional, physical, spiritual, or intellectual level.

SCOPE OF KERALA AS AN EXPERIENTIAL TOURISM HUB

Kerala, one of the ten paradises of the world as per National Geographic Travellers Magazine, is a top destination most travellers wish to visit. Though Kerala is one of the smallest states in India, Kerala is superabundant in tourist spots due to its unique culture, heritage, and varied topography. Hence Kerala has the prospective to offer an extensive array of experiential tourism activities. Kerala Tourism Development Corporation, the government agency is in charge of promoting and overseeing tourism activities of the State, laid the foundation for the growth of the tourism industry. Kerala, one of the destinations with the highest brand recall, is a popular destination for domestic and foreign tourists. The geography of Kerala is diverse, with landscapes ranging from mountains, coastal regions, evergreen forests to backwaters. Kerala also has varied culture, history, heritage, and pilgrim centres, making it the correct destination for all tourists. Some of the experiences Kerala offers as a tourist hub are as follows:

AYURVEDA

Kerala offers tourists an opportunity to comprehensively understand Ayurveda as a treatment form and as a tourist experience. Kerala has, since time immemorial, been the perfect host to practice Ayurveda and boasts of a wide range of Treatment and Research Centres. Rejuvenation Therapy, Panchakarma, unique treatments for various internal and external organs of the body are some services offered to tourists.

VILLAGE LIFE EXPERIENCE

More than just sightseeing, one can experience the essence of the villages of Kerala through this offer. Kalliasseri in Kannur, bell metal making of Kunnimangalam, Theyyam performances, pottery making, handicrafts and weaving villages are different aspects of Kerala that can get explored under village life experience.

ARTFORMS

Kerala has a plethora of art forms to offer to its guest. It can be classified into performing art forms like Kathakali, Kutiyattom; Ritual art forms like Theyyam, Patayani; Martial arts like Kalaripayyatu, Parisakali; and folk arts like Kolkali, Kummattikali.

RESPONSIBLE TOURISM

Responsible tourism is considered the brand that presents Kerala to tourists. Responsible Tourism Mission is the nodal agency to spread and implement the ideologies and initiatives of responsible tourism all over the State. It is a successful tool for the development and empowerment of villagers through the sustainable tourism model, encouraging community living through homestays, and promoting eco-living initiatives.

CUISINES

Spices of Kerala have attracted foreigners from centuries before. Be it offered in star restaurants or local tea stalls, the way it is prepared and served and the tastes offered through its cuisines create a memorable experience for tourists. Kerala meals, popularly known as Sadya, Spicy fish curry, toddy, etc., are some unique items Kerala offers its guests to experience.

MUSEUMS

The heritage and history of Kerala can be well-experienced museums. The history of Kerala depicts the ruling of Portuguese, Britishers and before the arrival of foreigners by the upper-class domestic residence of Samoothiris. Indo Portuguese museum, Keralam Museum of History and Heritage, Shaktan Thampuran Palace are some of the popular destinations for foreigners.

Apart from the above-mentioned, wildlife, hill stations, beaches, waterfall, and backwater also offers mesmerizing experiences to the visitors. The Kerala government has also recently launched caravan tourism to have a detailed understanding of the destinations mentioned above.

KERALA'S STREET MODEL IN EXPERIENTIAL TOURISM

In a pioneering initiative to take tourism deep into the state's interiors and rural hinterland, Kerala Tourism has launched the 'STREET' project in November 2021, which would help visitors' have an enhanced experience of the diversity of offerings in the villages of Kerala. The project is launched under the above-mentioned Responsible Tourism mission. The idea is inspired by the slogan of the United Nations World Tourism Organisation (UNWTO); ' Tourism for Inclusive Growth.' The STREET model will be introduced in seven places across Kerala at its initial phase. STREET stands for Sustainable, Tangible, Responsible, Experiential, Ethnic Tourism hubs. Diversified themes are introduced under this model to offer various experiences according to the visitors' taste under this project like green street, cultural street, village life experience street, experiential tourism street, agri-tourism street, water street, art street, etc. The STREET model can be an asset to the tourism sector of Kerala as it will foster mutually beneficial organic relationships between tourism development in the state and the ordinary lives of people. Other salient features of the STREET project are that it is implemented in the Public-Private Partnership mode and will have local bodies and residents of the selected locations as stakeholders.

ROLE OF EXPERIENTIAL TOURISM IN OFFERING BRAND EXPERIENCE

According to Hanna and Rowley (2011), a destination brand experience occurs when a person gains pleasurable experiences from a branded place. Most often, experiential tourism is associated with "authentic experiences". Rather than mass tourism being promoted, tourists nowadays try to seek more realistic and genuine experiences wherein they can closely interact and connect with a place's people, culture, or history. In Kerala, various possibilities offer tourists diverse experiences due to its vast culture, cuisine, natural beauty and many other factors.

The responsible tourism initiatives undertaken by Kerala Tourism Department requires special mention. Responsible tourism initiatives involve local people, making it possible for tourists to better understand local culture and activities through closer and more meaningful interactions with the local population. Through its Responsible Tourism Mission, Kerala offers various packages providing Cultural experiences, Village Life experiences, and Native experiences.

In the post-covid phase witnessed by the revival of the tourism business, every destination has to offer opportunities for authentic and genuine experiences for upcoming tourists. As already discussed, destination branding has assumed great relevance due to the high and growing competition in the field. Only places or destinations that can offer better experiences to the visitors will survive. The recent STREET project of Kerala Tourism is an example of offering such distinct opportunities' for tourists.

CONCLUSION

Kerala Tourism is trying to introduce experiential tourism in all the advantages. The recently introduced STREET project, Caravan Tourism, etc., are all examples of the same. While doing the same, Kerala has to consider inculcating brand experience to experiential tourism to enhance its existing 'Brand Kerala'. As discussed above, a brand can be experienced in various dimensions like sensory, affective, intellectual and behavioural experiences. Each dimension has a varied impact. Beaches and hill stations may be offering a sensory brand experience, whereas museums may be offering some intellectual brand experience. Kerala Tourism Department and researchers should study the impact of offering such a variety of experiential tourism packages on brand experience for effective branding of Kerala as a destination brand.

REFERENCES

- Barnes, S.J., Mattsson, J. and Sørensen, F. (2014),"Destination brand experience and visitor behavior: Testing a scale in the tourism context", Annals of Tourism Research, Vol. 48, pp. 121-139.
- Brakus, J. J., Schmitt, B. H., & Zarantonello, L. (2009). Brand experience: What is it? How is it measured? Does it affect loyalty?. Journal of Marketing, 73, 52–68.
- Cai, L. (2002). Cooperative branding for rural destinations. Annals of Tourism Research, 29(3), 720-742
- Hanna, S. & Rowley, J. (2011). Towards a Strategic Place Brand-management Model. Journal of Marketing Management, 27 (5-6): 458-76.
- Rajan, R. B. (2015). Experiential Tourism: Understanding Tourism Trends Today To Prepare for Tomorrow. Shanlax International Journal of Commerce, 3(1), 2320–4168
- Experience Kerala
- https://www.keralatourism.org/specialities/
- Responsible Tourism
- https://www.keralatourism.org/responsible-tourism/experience
- UNWTO - Glossary of Tourism Terms
- https://www.unwto.org/glossary-tourism-terms

CHAPTER 2

GLIMPSES OF RURAL TOURISM IN INDIA AND KERALA

Lt. Seena V.
Assistant Professor of Economics
TKMM College Nangiarkulangara

Dr. Sheela M.C.
Associate Professor of Economics & Research Guide
University College Thiruvananthapuram

INTRODUCTION

In India, rural tourism is an emerging concept. The pressures of urban life and the alienation and distance from the natural environment often force city dwellers to escape from their lonely and monotones city life. In such cases, they feel that the rural location is an ideal place to release stress and to re-engage in a simple lifestyle that provides rest and complete peace for a period of time. Not only that, but also such tourism is widely accepted because it can shape up the rural community by providing financial and social benefits. Although the concept is relatively new one and it has recently gained immense importance around the world.

India is a land of villages. A large section of India's population living in rural areas is still traditionally dependent on agriculture and allied activities. However, the income from agriculture is declining day by day and these villagers do not have adequate alternative employment opportunities. This situation motivates them to settle in nearby urban areas in search of better income, employment and better livelihood. If rural India can be rebuilt, rejuvenated and promoted as tourist destinations, these villagers can certainly get adequate number of alternative jobs, can possibly reduce the tendency to leave the native villages and in such way the socio-economic condition of rural India can also be improved.

Keywords: Rural tourism, Farm Tourism, Agritourism, Adventure tourism, Heritage tourism, Responsible tourism Mission, Swadesh Darshan, Human

Resource Directory, STREET Project, PEPPER Project, Hunar Se Rozgar Tak

RURAL TOURISM IN INDIA

India, a land of diversity, offers a lot to tourists. Rural tourism in India is still in its infancy, but once its full potential is fully utilized, tourists and rural people alike can benefit from each other. Each region, each state and each village in our country has its own language, culture, traditions, customs, costumes and cuisines that will provide a memorable experience for tourists. Therefore Mahatma Gandhi once said that "India lives in its villages". The village life in India is where you meet the **'real India'**. These villages are also a storehouse of the culture and heritage of the country.

Rural Tourism offers many opportunities for tourists to experience the wonders of nature and showcase the true beauty of rural India. Rural tourism helps to strengthen the rural economy and alleviate poverty to some extent by developing infrastructure and creating employment opportunities for the local people. Rural tourism activities promote the conservation of biodiversity and the preservation of local heritage in terms of arts and crafts and thus cultivate a sense of pride among the rural people.

In the rural area, practitioners of unique arts and crafts are in their original form, which is hard to find in cities. However, most of the rural people depend on agrarian and allied occupation for their livelihood. Their income is not as good as in cities. There are not many jobs available in many villages and many young men and women are migrating to the cities in search of better opportunities. This led to the gradual decline of some of the arts and crafts traditionally practiced in rural communities. Rural tourism is one of the solutions to all the above problems. If rural India can be rebuilt, rejuvenated and promoted as tourist destinations, these villagers can certainly get adequate number of alternative jobs, can possibly reduce the tendency to leave the native villages and in such way the socio-economic condition of rural India can also be improved. Rural tourism focuses on the visitor who actively participates in the rural lifestyle. The tourist travels to a rural area and enjoys life while participating in the daily activities of the village. Here, tourists get a chance to experience the traditions, culture and unique way of life of the region. The local community also benefits from the change in their occupations, which depend on agriculture or low-skilled occupations, as a way to increase income. They can incorporate other cultures of visitors and thus expand their knowledge and horizons.

RURAL TOURISM IN KERALA

The spirit of Kerala resides in the rustic landscapes of the villages that evoke new experiences for every visitor. Village life in God's own country is rich in innumerable traditions, cultures and art. Kerala was the first region to adopt the concept of developing and promoting rural tourism. Relevantly, Kerala is one of the most popular eco destinations. For example, the Kumarakom Rural Tourism Project in Kerala showed the country how to benefit the local community by ensuring eco-friendly activities and nature conservation. Under this scheme, Kerala Tourism has entered into an agreement with Kudumbasree to sell fruits and vegetables purchased from locals at kiosks and to distribute them to hotels and restaurants. Kerala has won the Best Award for Rural Tourism in this eco-friendly tourism model.

The concept of Rural or Village Life Experience in the field of tourism was first introduced by the Responsible Tourism Mission. It was brought forward with the objective of preserving the traditional handicrafts, traditional occupations and rural life of Kerala. The main highlight of the concept is that it ensures public participation in tourism development and thereby supports farmers, small entrepreneurs and traditional artisans. Currently, the Village Life Experience of the Responsible Tourism Mission is a model that has won praise and acclaim around the world.

Responsible Tourism has introduced a number of innovative tour packages as part of its rural tourism experience. RT Mission has decided to introduce tour packages including weaving centers at Kallyassery in Kannur, gem metal making at Kunjimangalam, various theyyams, visits to agricultural areas and traditional fishing methods.Work is in progress on new Cultural Tour Packages, Festival Packages, Tent Accommodation Experience Packages, Heritage Tour Packages, Carbon Free Packages, Farming & Craft Village Packages, and Story Telling Packages.

Currently, RT Mission packages are available at all major tourist destinations in Kerala including Kumarakom, Wayanad, Thekkady, Kannur, Bekal, Alappuzha and Thiruvananthapuram. In Kumarakom RT Mission currently offers two Rural Life Experience packages: A Day with Farmers and Beyond the Backwaters. It provides a variety of folk experiences including- coconut climbing, screw pine, coconut leaf weaving, pottery making, boating, fishing, rope making, farm and paddy field visits. Wayanad is a paradise of rich heritage and culture of its unique tribal communities. RT Mission currently offers 4 spellbinding experiences in Wayanad, including: A Day at Chetyalathoor, Cheruvayal, Nellarachal and Thekkumthara.

OBJECTIVES OF THE STUDY

1. To make clear the concept of 'Rural Tourism'

2. To identify different forms of Rural Tourism

3. To understand the benefits and issues of Rural Tourism in Indian and Kerala context

4. To present major initiates for the promotion of rural tourism development.

MEANING OF RURAL TOURISM

Rural tourism means any form of tourism that showcases the rural life, culture, heritage and art in rural areas, thereby benefiting the local community economically and socially, enabling a richer tourism experience between tourists and local people. Rural tourism is an activity that mainly takes place in rural areas. It is multifaceted and may include agricultural tourism, farm tourism, nature tourism, cultural tourism, adventure tourism and eco-tourism. In contrast to traditional tourism, rural tourism has some special features; it is experience based, tourism places are sparsely populated, it is mainly in harmony with nature, it meshes with seasonality and local events and is based on the preservation of culture, heritage and traditions. Rural tourism is defined as the movement of people from a normal residential area to a rural area for a minimum of twenty - four hours and a maximum of six months for the purpose of leisure and pleasure. In other words rural tourism refers to all the tourism activities in a rural area.

The concept of rural tourism is defined in many ways and is subject to number of interpretations.

The United Nations World Tourism Organization (UNWTO) defines rural tourism as "a type of tourism activity in which the visitor's experience is related to a wide range of products generally linked to nature-based activities, agriculture, rural lifestyle/culture, angling and sightseeing".

The **OECD** states rural tourism should be:

➤ Located in rural areas.

➤ Functionally rural, built upon the rural world's special features; small-scale enterprises, open space, contact with nature and the natural world, heritage, traditional societies, and traditional practices.

➤ Rural in scale – both in terms of building and settlements – and therefore, small scale.

➤ Traditional in character, growing slowly and organically, and connected with local families.

➤ Sustainable – in the sense that its development should help sustain the special rural character of an area, and in the sense that its development should be sustainability in its use of resources.

➤ Thus Rural Tourism refers to the tourism that takes tourists to experience "the actual culture" of a rural setting.

Ministry of Tourism, Government of India defines it as "any form of tourism that showcases the rural life, art, culture, and heritage at rural locations, thereby benefiting the local community economically and socially as well as enabling interaction between the tourists and the locals for a more enriching tourism experience can be termed as rural tourism".

According to Das and Nilanjay (2014) the basic motivation for visiting rural areas is to understand the lifestyle of rural residents. Recognizing its business potential, the suburbs of the metropolitan cities of Delhi, Mumbai, Jaipur, Chennai and Kolkata have developed some rural tourist attractions for weekend visitors, where they are presented with bullock cart rides, crops, plows, mud baths and milking. Many tourists flock to these areas, which contribute to the rural economy by staying at home in the countryside, eating local delicacies and buying local handicrafts.

FORMS OF RURAL TOURISM

Rural tourism is considered as an umbrella term. It includes a number of tourism types, such as

1. **Agritourism:** It involves the visit of tourists to an agriculture farm or a ranch; especially those tourists who have a keen interest in how food is produced. Tourists are encouraged to learn about farming

practices while visiting these farms. It includes farm stays (stays of tourists at bed and breakfast (B&B) on farms), cheese making, feeding animals, riding horses, picking fruits and vegetables directly from the trees and the farms, shopping and learning about farm produce and agricultural processes. There will be an opportunity to see the lifestyles of farmers and realizing the advantages of staying in the countryside.

2. **Eco tourism**: Eco-tourism is a nature based tourism activity, which refers to the process of visiting natural areas for the purpose of enjoying the scenery, including plant and animal wildlife. At the same time it does not disturbing the integrity of the ecosystem and creating economic opportunities that make conservation and protection of natural resources and advantageous to local people. It can be one of the medium to preserve local culture, flora and fauna and other natural resources.

3. **Adventure tourism**: Adventure tourism is the process of exploring or travelling to remote, exotic and hostile areas. Adventure tourism is very popular among young tourists and allows tourists to step outside of their comfort zone. Adventure tourism require considerable effort and, to a certain extent, risk and physical danger. Activities include mountaineering, trekking, bungee jumping, mountain biking, river rafting and rock climbing. With its diverse landscape and climate, India offers a lot of potential for adventure tourism.

4. **Farm Tourism**: In India, the state of Haryana pioneered in initiating the concept of farmhouses and farm stays. Being away from the hustle and bustle of urban life and to find tranquillity are the main mottos of such tourists who visit farms and stay in farmhouses. Participating in farm activities such as engaging in plucking orchids, taking cattle rides, mud bathing, tasting honey, horseback riding, taking bullock cart rides or tractor rides, feeding cattle, going for herbal excursions, participation in organic farming and growing crops are some of the activities that the tourists may look forward to while staying in the farmhouses.

5. **Heritage tourism**: Heritage tourism is defined as "travel undertaken to explore and experience places, activities, and artifacts that authentically represent the stories and people of the past and present". It is based on the cultural heritage of the tourist location.

India is famous for its rich heritage and ancient culture. The rich heritage of the country is reflected in the various temples, majestic forts, amusement parks, religious monuments, museums, art galleries and rural sites which are the strongholds of civilization. All these structures are products of heritage tourism.

6. **Wildlife Tourism:** Wildlife tourism, one of the fastest growing areas of tourism, involves travelling to different places to experience wildlife in natural conditions. India is rich in flora and fauna, rich in birds, mammals, reptiles, amphibians, plants and animals. To take advantage of the potential of wildlife tourism, the government has launched some wildlife packages for travelers. Wildlife tourism in India includes wildlife photography, bird watching, jungle safaris, elephant safaris, jeep safaris, jungle camping, trekking and hiking.

BENEFITS OF RURAL TOURISM

Rural offers many benefits to the rural community. Rural tourism contributes to the development of rural areas and the quality of life of the host communities. Some of the benefits of rural tourism are:

➤ Provides new, alternative or related source of income and employment in rural areas.

➤ Rural tourism promotes infrastructure development in rural areas.

➤ Revives local culture.

➤ Raise the standard of living of the local community.

➤ Fosters a sense of local pride, self-esteem and personality.

➤ Contributes to the conservation of natural resources and the environment.

➤ Preservation of Local Culture and tradition.

➤ The local community members start learning new skill.

➤ Cultural exchange

➤ Women empowerment

➤ Entrepreneurship opportunities

ISSUES OF RURAL TOURISM

The major issues and challenges of rural tourism are the need for environmental protection, natural resources, the need for education, the proper understanding of tourists and locals, and the need to create a democratic movement that will enable people at all levels to participate in tourism development. Some of the major issues of rural tourism are:

- Financial leakage
- Local inflation
- Destroy indigenous culture.
- Build or distort local 'culture' for commodity and stage authenticity.
- Destruction of natural habitats of rural wildlife.
- Waste disposal, discharge, and other forms of pollution
- Congestion
- Distort the local employment structure.

MAJOR INITIATIVES TO PROMOTE RURAL TOURISM IN INDIA AND KERALA

1. **Swadesh Darshan Scheme**: Recognizing the potential of rural tourism in the country, the Ministry of Tourism has launched the Swadesh Darshan Scheme for the integrated development of theme based tourist circuits for the development of tourism infrastructure across the country. The Ministry of Tourism has identified the Rural Circuit as one of the 15 thematic circuits identified for development under this project. The objectives of the Swadesh Darshan project are to create employment opportunities through the active involvement of local communities, to promote community based development and to promote a pro-poor tourism approach. Under the Swadesh Darshan scheme, 77 projects have been sanctioned of worth Rs. 6,035.70 crore (US$ 863.60 million). In Union Budget 2020-21, the Government has allotted Rs. 1,200 crore (US$ 171.70 million) for the development of tourist circuits for Northeast. The Ministry has sanctioned 80.37 crore for the development of rural circuits under this Scheme and for the development of Malanad Malabar Cruise Tourism in Kerala.

2. **National Rurban Mission (NRuM)**: National Rurban Mission (NRuM)

formerly known as Shyama Prasad Mukherji Rurban Mission (SPMRM). The Rurban Mission follows the vision of "Development of a cluster of villages that preserve and nurture the essence of rural community life with focus on equity and inclusiveness without compromising with the facilities perceived to be essentially urban in nature, thus creating a cluster of "Rurban villages".

3. **Product Infrastructure Development at Destinations and Circuits (PIDDC)**: The aim of this project is to showcase rural life, art, culture and heritage in the villages. Central financial assistance (CFA) up to 50.00 lakh is provided for arts, handicrafts, handlooms, textiles and natural environment. The project provides financial assistance for infrastructure development, capacity building, solid waste treatment and fresh water supply. The project also aims to harness the full potential of the tourism sector by improving infrastructure.

4. **Domestic Promotion and Publicity including Hospitality (DPPH) scheme**: For the promotion of rural tourism, the Department of Tourism has been providing financial assistance to the State Governments and UT Governments through the DPPH scheme for organizing tourism related events such as fairs / festivals, seminars, conclaves and conventions. Under DPPH scheme, the Ministry of Tourism is implementing various measures to promote tourism in the country. The main objective of the DPPH project is to create a general awareness among the local people about the potential tourist destinations in the country which will help to enhance the local or domestic tourism market. Under the scheme, the Ministry promotes printing, advertising in electronic media, participation in fairs and exhibitions, organizing seminars, organizing workshops for participants and service providers, printing of brochures and collaterals.

5. **Hunar Se Rozgar Tak (HSRT) / Capacity Building for Service Providers**: As part of the Suo-Motu initiatives of the Ministry of Tourism under the Scheme of "Capacity Building for Service Providers", it was decided to provide financial assistance to Government sponsored Tourism & Hospitality Institutes, Private Tourism/Hospitality Institutes, State Tourism Development Corporations and State Governments etc. to conduct Skill Development Programmes to be called "HUNAR SE ROZGAR" or its verticals. Under this scheme trainees are trained for

jobs such as guide, driver, cook, housekeeping and hospitality.

6. **PEPPER (People's Participation for Participatory Planning & Empowerment):** PEPPER is a revolutionary tourism venture of Kerala Tourism under the Responsible Tourism Mission. It is the process of finding and developing new tourist destinations in rural areas with the support of the local community and local self-governing bodies (LSG). Through this initiative, grassroots level community participation is ensured from the very beginning of the initial discussions. Kerala Tourism is perhaps the first in the world to bring such a participatory tourism approach to the country. This project was first implemented in Vaikom taluk of Kottayam district.

7. **STREET Project:** Kerala Tourism launched the 'STREET' project to promote and take tourism deep into the interiors and rural hinterland of Kerala. The project helps visitors to experience the diversity of tourism products in these areas. The STREET is an acronym for Sustainable, Tangible, Responsible, Experiential, Ethnic, Tourism hubs. Green street, cultural street, village life experience street, experiential tourism street, agri-tourism street, water street and art street are the themes that have been planned as part of the project.

8. **Human Resource Directory:** RT Mission promotes activities that bring greater economic benefits to the local people and enhance their well-being. One of such Mission is the Human Resource Directory. The HR Directory aims to connect skilled and unskilled workers to the tourism sector. It includes a detailed list of people working in Panchayats, Kudumbasree units, tourism educational institutions, labour groups and employment schemes. Job seekers can register on this platform at any time.

CONCLUSION

India, a country of diversity, offers a lot to tourists. Rural tourism in India is still in its infancy stage, but once its full potential is utilized, it will benefit tourists and rural people alike. Each region, each state and each village in our country has its own language, culture, traditions, customs, costumes and cuisines that will provide unforgettable experiences to the tourists. That is why Mahatma Gandhi emphasized that India lives in villages and that only through their rural development can India regain its glory and prosperity.

REFERENCES

- Seena, V. and Sheela, M.C. (2021) Rural Economy of India in the eve of COVID 19, Infinity Indica Publishers, 48-61.
- Nagaraju, L.G. Chandrashekara, B. (2014), 'Rural Tourism and Rural Development in India' International Journal of Interdisciplinary and Multidisciplinary Studies (IJIMS), Vol 1, No.6, 42-48.
- Bhattacharya, R. and Kolhi, S. (2008), 'Promoting Rural and Village Tourism for Urban Families', Conference on Tourism in India-Challenges Ahead, IIMK. 15-17 May.
- Gopal, R., Varma, S. and Gopinathan, R. (2008), 'Rural Tourism Development: Constraints and Possibilities with a Special Reference to Agri Tourism-A Case Study on Agri Tourism Destinations, Conference on Tourism in India- Challenges Ahead, IIMK, 15-17 May.
- Suzanne, W. Dainiel, R. Fesenmaier, Julie Fesenmaier and John C. (2001), 'Factors for Success in Rural Tourism Development', Journal of Travel Research, Vol. 40, P. 132.
- Wanda George, E. Heather Mair and Donald G. Reid 'Rural Tourism Development
- Localism and Cultural Change' (2009), Channel View Publications, St Nicholas House, 31–34 High Street, Bristol BS1 2AW, UK.
- Kurukshetra A Journal On Rural Development Vol. 67 No. 6 April 2019.
- https://tourism.gov.in/
- https://www.keralatourism.org/responsible-tourism/
- https://www.jkpi.org/the-way-to-eco-friendly-tourism-is-through-rural-tourism/
- https://www.keralatourism.org/responsible-tourism/village-life-experience/12
- http://www.swaniti.com/wp-content/uploads/2015/11/Developing-Rural-Tourism.pdf
- https://www.smartgovernance.in/government-takes-initiatives-to-promote-rural-tourism/

CHAPTER 3

IMPACT OF COVID 19 ON PILGRIMAGE TOURISM: A STUDY WITH SPECIAL REFERENCE TO SABARIMALA

Minu Rose Francis
Assistant Professor,
Amal Jothi College of Engineering,
Koovappally

ABSTRACT

The Indian tourism sector is blessed with a lot of important religious destinations. Pilgrimages to these destinations help in bringing the various benefits to the host destination in terms of economic growth, regional development, and destination planning. Sabarimala Sree Dhamma Sastha temple, dedicated to Lord Ayyappa is one of the most famous and prominent among all the temples in Kerala. The number of pilgrims visiting the famous Sabarimala temple in the Pathanamthitta district of Kerala is very huge. During the pandemic period, this flow of tourists was limited due to the entry restriction and related aspects. However, the post-pandemic period is witnessing a revival. The present study attempts to investigate the role of pilgrimage tourism in Sabarimala and its positive externalities. Moreover, What India or World can learn from this model? The paper is designed based on the conceptual research and qualitative technique using the questionnaire and secondary data is collected by reviewing various articles relating to the Sabarimala Pilgrimage Tourism in Kerala. The present study is carried out to know the impact of Pilgrimage Tourism, what all things we can adapt, change, and the integrated development of the destination for better tourism promotion in the Pathanamthitta District of Kerala.

Keywords: Pilgrimage Tourism, Economic Growth, Sabarimala Model, Regional Development

INTRODUCTION

Pilgrimage tourism can be found under the clause of religious tourism, spiritual tourism, or sacred tourism with a vision of travel for religious or spiritual purposes, and exploring the religious monuments and artifacts associated with it. Nowadays people find religious places more preferable as tourism destinations. Pilgrimage tourism is conquering the tourism industry as it can contribute to spiritual and mental wellbeing especially in this kind of era of depression and pressures. The major impact of every kind of tourism is nothing but the elimination of infrastructural bottlenecks. The roads and means of transport became more efficient and return-oriented. Regional development and employment opportunities, economic growth of the region in particular, and state, in general, are also something which one should not miss out. As per the report of official sources, uncertainty over the extension of the pandemic-induced disruptions marked a slowdown in the pace of growth of pilgrim tourism in every sphere.

SABARIMALA

Kerala, God's own country, is famous as a tourist-prone area and spotted for pilgrim tourism. Sabarimala, the 'Sacred Abode of Lord Ayyappa' is one of the most visited prominent Hindu pilgrim centres in the country. Sabarimala is located on a hilltop in Kerala's Pathanamthitta district. It is located in a place, surrounded by 18 hills in the Periyar Tiger Reserve. The temple attracts pilgrims from various parts of the country especially from Kerala, Karnataka, Tamil Nadu, and Andra. The temple is open for worship only during the days of Mandala Pooja in November-December,

Makara Sankranti on January 14 and Maha Vishuva Sankranti on April 14, and the first five days of each Malayalam month. Even though Sabarimala is an ancient temple, people could hardly be reached there due to infrastructural bottlenecks especially in the form of transportation hardships. It was in the 12th century, Manikandan, the prince of the Pandalam Dynasty has rediscovered the proper route to the temple. The prince is assumed to be an incarnation of Lord Ayyappa. He has been followed by a lot of descendants including the Vavar's.

Erumeli Vavar Mosque, which is a holy place for both Hindus and Muslims deserves attention while thinking about Sabarimala. The mosque is situated very close to an Ayappa temple and, irrespective of their caste and religion, people who visit Sabarimala would definitely visit the mosque dedicated to Vavarswami, before proceeding on their journey.

This temple located in the Pathanamthitta district is 70 kilometers far from Pathanamthitta and 161km from cochin and 208 kilometers from Thiruvananthapuram. The state's ambitious Sabari rail plan, a proposes111 km railway line from Angamaly to Erumeli, with Kerala Rail Development Corporation (K-rail) is expected to start rolling soon. The Greenfield airport proposed for this means also acts as a reference for future prospects of pilgrimage tourism to Sabarimala.

OBJECTIVES

1.   To study the impact of covid 19 on pilgrimage tourism

2.   To understand the socio-economic impact of covid on Sabarimala

3.   To find the policies and measures of pilgrimage tourism

METHODOLOGY

The study uses both Qualitative and Quantitative. The primary data was collected through random sampling from 40 units and secondary data include study reports, newspaper articles using previous studies are involved in this area of research

LIMITATION OF THE STUDY

There was a time constraint. Even though we have secondary data, it was limited due to covid restrictions.

IMPACT OF COVID 19 ON SABARIMALA PILGRIMAGE TOURISM

Pilgrimage tourism is exploring the world of tourism today. Sabarimala temple is one of the prominent temples that fetches a great share of revenue to the Kerala economy. Covid 19 evidently revealed its externalities on the tourism industry as it is on other industries. The level of income, employment, and growth has shown a tremendous slowdown. The positive spillovers too demand attention as the parallel shift of procedures online and introduced new online portal and promotion of activities like virtual queues and all.

ENVIRONMENT AND ECOLOGY

Punyam poonkavanam: this initiative of cleaning drives at Sabarimala with VIPs joining the public for cleaning the accumulated waste at the holy place every morning during the pilgrim season.

Another feature that cannot be eliminated is the positive impact on the environment as the pollution range came to a drastic decline. River Pamba is a major source of drinking eater for Pathanamthitta natives. The water quality in the Pamba river got deteriorated as a result of waste and the presence of e coli and coliforms were detected. The pandemic and resultant restrictions played a positive role in bringing back the quality of water and reducing water pollution due to pH, TDS, Total acidity, Total alkalinity, Total hardness, Chloride are within the limit. The value of turbidity is high compared to the values before pilgrimage season.

Sabarimala before and after covid pandemic

HEALTH CARE

The system of health care services in Sabarimala temple is something that deserves appreciation.

Medical College Hospital Kottayam, General Hospital Pathanamthitta, Cardiology centers at Pampa, Neelimala, Appachimedu, and Sannidhanam are some of the hospitals where the Pilgrims can seek medical care. There are two mobile units each at Pampa & Nilakkal with emergency facilities.

During the pandemic, those who were diagnosed with the disease and those who were included in the primary contact list were removed from Sannidhanam in a timely manner. "Despite the staff being affected, an alternative system was put in place to carry out the pilgrimage

Prior to the pandemic outbreak, the health services of Sabarimala were focused on cardiac arrests, heart attacks, pressure issues, disasters, problems as a result of being trapped in the crowd. Now the health facilities adapted their services to meet the covid affected pilgrims, quarantine, and all other related necessary activities.

INCOME

Sabarimala pilgrimage tourism was found to be one of the major sources of income for the state as well. Before the outbreak of pandemic

The income of Sabarimala marked a drain last year followed by a reduction in the number of pilgrims to less than 5 percentage.

As we all know, return is always accompanied by some investments. 2019 Kerala budget has given a good proportion of its expenditure for Sabarimala and related projects. Rs 739 crore was allotted for the overall development of Sabarimala. Major development projects were announced in the Kerala budget. According to Travancore Devaswom Board (TDB) officials, the sale of Appam and Aravana, to be given as prasadham and the collections through donation boxes accounted for the majority of revenue. The plan to lease out the rest of the stalls at the Sannidhanam too witnessed an improved response with the rise in pilgrim flow. The overall income during the two-month season last year, which was severely scaled back due to COVID-19, was just 21 crore

The pandemic results are evident as "Of the 216 stalls, 101 have been auctioned off, although at much lesser rates. As per the data revealed by TDB, the income of the Sabarimala met a contraction during the first 39 days of the Sabarimala season in 2020 has fallen to Rs 9.09 crore from Rs 156.60 crore in the same period in 2019 due to restrictions imposed as a result of COVID-19 pandemic. With the easing and liberalizing of pandemic-related restrictions and increase in daily slots for darshan, pilgrims at Sabarimala and the revenue collection were also on a rise parallelly.

The Devasom Board is expecting that the revenue collection will be able to make a quantum jump once the Government permits overnight stay at the Sannidhanam while considering the physical hardship and efforts involved in forcing pilgrims to trek up and down the hillock within a few hours. The revenue can be raised by introducing new provisions for accommodation.

Also, there are certain hindrances in the form of infrastructure bottlenecks followed by torrential rain and related flood. The services including health and safety are something that can be adopted by others. Kerala's approach towards the covid pandemic was also commendable. The mode of identifying and tracing the covid patients and those who had contacts with them gained world attention. In the case of Sabarimala in particular, despite the staff, those who were affected an alternative system was introduced to carry out the pilgrimage.

The pandemic can be described as the latest in a series of unfortunate events that had been impacting the TDB adversely over the past few years. The Board had incurred a huge setback in 2018-19, in the wake of violent protests by some Hindu organizations following the Supreme Court order on September 28, 2018, allowing women of all ages to enter the hill shrine. The floods had also inflicted a blow on its income.

FINDINGS OF THE STUDY

1. The findings of the study are mentioned below

2. The revenue from Sabarimala Pilgrimage tourism has declined drastically.

3. Introduction of Digitalization in the form of the virtual queue.

4. The quality of water in the Pampa River shows improvement and water pollution also depicts a commendable decline.

5. Health care facilities are well maintained and provided for quarantine and covid protocols are well maintained.

6. The master plan to develop Sabarimala with respect to infrastructure, environmental sustainability, and pilgrim facilities can result in a great and substantiate change that can transform Sabarimala into a role model for other pilgrimage tourism spots.

7. Digitalization made the procedures more systematic and transparent. It also remained a hindrance for those who are under the digital divide.

Conclusion

Sabarimala pilgrimage tourism has been emerging as an ideal model for pilgrimage tourism considering its performance in different perspectives. Even though the outbreak of covid 19 influenced the Sabarimala pilgrimage worst in terms of income, its positive spillovers deserve attention. The water quality in the Pampa River increased, the air became cleaner and the pollution also declined to a great extent. Moreover, digitalization has been introduced into Sabarimala pilgrimage tourism in the form of virtual queues and so on. Kerala got appreciated by the World Health organization in terms of its approach toward pandemics. Similarly, Sabarimala also acts as a model in its approach to the pandemic situation. All these initiatives are concentrated on human development and quality of life rather than revenue prospects. More specifically Sabarimala followed the path of Kerala in upholding the quality in terms of social, cultural, and economic terms.

The study is aimed at identifying the scope of Sabarimala, being a model to all other pilgrimage tourism centers, and gaining the world's attention. There is an opportunity for its future prospects and the Mater plan mentioned in the portal is aiming towards a world-class transformation including trekking path, riverfront, rail, and air services, etc. the model of Sabarimala should emphasize on infrastructural development, ecological sustainability, and pilgrim facilities

GLOSSARY

1. Pilgrimage Tourism: Pilgrimage is an ancient form of mobility and a fundamental precursor to modern tourism. Traditionally, it applies to journeys with a religious purpose, but it can also refer to secular travel with particular importance for the pilgrim (Morinis 1992).

2. Infrastructural bottlenecks: can be the outcome of chronic or temporary conditions. Physical restrictions can form bottlenecks as traffic expands, such as a bridge or a port.

3. Travancore Devasom Board: Travancore Devaswom Board is an autonomous body constituted under the Travancore Cochin Hindu Religious Institutions Act XV of 1950.

4. Prasadham: it is a food offering to a deity, later distributed to worshippers

5. Master plan: a comprehensive Sabarimala master plan has been prepared (by IL&FS-Ecosmart) with the objectives of planned overall development

6. Digitalization: use of digital technologies like online booking, virtual queue etc.

7. Digital divide: lack of internet facilities

REFERENCES

> (Bg) Impact of Pilgrimage Tourism with Special reference to Sabarimala, Pathanamthitta, Kerala

> *www. Kerala tourism.gov.in*

> http://timesofindia.indiatimes.com/articleshow/67768523.cms?utm_source=contentofinteres

> "ministry of Tourism,2020." n.d.

> *Subha Lekshmi, Athira Somarajan, Merlin Daniel, Vishak Sasidhar, 2020, Water Quality Analysis of River PAMBA using WQI Method and GIS Mapping, INTERNATIONAL JOURNAL OF ENGINEERING RESEARCH & TECHNOLOGY (IJERT) Volume 09, Issue 06 (June 2020),*

> Role of Tourism Industry in India's Development: Sultan Singh Jaswals

CHAPTER 4

SOCIO-ECONOMIC AND ECOLOGICAL IMPACT OF TOURISM AFTER AFFECTING CORONA-

WITH SPECIAL REFERENCE TO TOURISM IN MUNNAR.

Lincy Koshy
Guest Faculty,
Dept. of Economics,
Bishop Abraham Memorial College, Thuruthicad.

ABSTRACT

Tourism is one of the world's major economic sectors and the third-largest export category and in 2019 accounted for 7% of global trade.One of the sectors most affected by the Covid-19 pandemic is tourism which further impacting economies, livelihoods, public services and opportunities on all continents. All parts of its vast value-chain have been affected. Kerala is one of the State which is vehemently affected with COVID 19 pandemic on its tourism sector. This study analysis the socio- economic impact of the pandemic on Munnar tourism and various policy measures taken to boost the tourism industry.

Key words: Tourism, Socio - Economic Impact, Ecology, Migrant workers, COVID-19 Pandemic, Air quality index.

INTRODUCTION

Tourism is one of the leading sectors of almost all economies in the world which contributes large scale employment, infrastructure, and cultural exchange between regions. Tourism is one of the world's major economic sectors. It is the third-largest export category (after fuels and chemicals) and in 2019 accounted for 7% of global trade (UNWTO). The COVID-19 had put drastic impacts on the global socio-economic, political and cultural spheres. The advent of the pandemic had stricken the tourism and its allied sectors very badly. Health communication strategies like social distancing, lockdown, travel and mobility ban,stay at home campaigns, break the chain campaign, self or mandatory quarantine had seriously impacted the global as well as regional tourism. (Sigala) As per the estimates, Global Travel and Tourism sector suffered a loss of almost US$4.5 trillion to reach US$4.7 trillion in 2020. In 2019, the Travel & Tourism sector contributed 10.4% to global GDP which is further decreased to 5.5% in 2020 due to ongoing restrictions to mobility. In 2020, 62 million jobs were lost, representing a drop of 18.5%, leaving just 272 million employed across the sector globally, compared to 334 million in 2019. The threat of job losses persists as many jobs are currently supported by government retention schemes and reduced hours, which without a full recovery of Travel & Tourism could be lost. Domestic visitor spending decreased by 45%, while international visitor spending declined by an unprecedented 69.4%.

India is one of the top travel destinations of foreigners. As a land of diversity, India's tourism sector is providing a pack of diverse experience to its tourists. In WTTC's Economic Impact 2019 report, India's Travel & Tourism GDP contribution grew by 4.9%, which was the third highest after China and Philippines. Additionally, the report also highlights that between 2014-2019, India witnessed the strongest growth in the number of jobs created (6.36 million), followed by China (5.47 million) and the Philippines (2.53 million). (India Brand Equity Foundation)

Kerala, which is always a traveler's paradise also called God's own Country,which is abundantly blessed with natural beauty and greenery. Kerala Tourism has gained a lot of tourist from all over the world, especially from UK, USA, France, Germany, Saudi Arabia and Australia. Kerala Tourism is to position itself as a global destination for tourism which is based on the advantage of the local resources, thereby attracting investment and resulting into sustainable development for the people of Kerala. An equable climate, a long shoreline with serene beaches, tranquil stretches of emerald backwaters, lush hill stations and exotic wildlife, waterfalls, sprawling plantations and paddy fields, enchanting art forms, magical festivals, historic and cultural monuments, exotic cuisine, all of which makes Kerala a unique experience.

Kerala has been well known for hundreds of years for its practice of Ayurveda, the traditional health science of India. People from all over the world comes to kerala as apart of Ayurvedic treatment and to heal with the nature itself. The backwaters of Kerala are a unique product of state and is found nowhere else in the world. Backwaters are a network of lakes, canals and estuaries and deltas of forty-four rivers that drain into the Arabian sea.. The Kerala Backwaters offer a spectacular opportunity to see Kerala and are easily traversed by boat. Houseboat rentals are very popular with honeymooners.

Kerala is one of the prominent landscapes which attracts tourists from all over the world. As tagged "God's own country", Kerala's tourism had changed its socio-economic panorama. Tourism industry contributes to 10 percent of State GDP and contributes 23.5 percent to the total employment of the state. Foreign as well as Domestic tourist prefer Kerala as their travel destination in terms of leisure and business-related visits. Kerala is one among the dream destination of global tourists. The success of the Tourism industry was appreciated by many National and International agencies, which include Pacific Asia Travel Association (PATA) Award for Women 's Empowerment, and the Travel Advertisement Broadcast Media and Website award in 2019. The State also received the PATA Gold Awards 2018 for the Best Honeymoon Destination in India, the Lonely Planet Travel Award for Best Destination for Families 2018, and the World Travel Mart Gold Award 2018 for Responsible Tourism and Managing Success in Tourism. Kerala Tourism also won national-level awards such as the National Tourism Award (2018) for Wayanad Responsible Tourism Project under the Category Best Responsible Tourism Project, and Outstanding Achievement Award for Responsible Tourism Mission at the Indian Responsible Tourism Awards

As a most chosen travel destination, Kerala even facing lots of difficulty in allocating basic infrastructure and other facilities. Kerala is in the top of tourism and allied activities when compared to any other Indian states, as the same reason the global pandemic shattered the entire prosperity of this sector. Nationwide lockdowns, break the chain campaigns, travel and community mob restrictions, stay at home and cancelling of aircrafts, in order to reduce the pandemic, spread hit the tourism sector very much also had impacted the economy on a large scale.

MUNNAR

Munnar is one of top destination in Kerala for domestic as well as foreign tourists. The origin of the place name Munnar traces to three mountain streams merge - Mudrapuzha, Nallathanni and Kundala. Munnar is located in the Western Ghats of Kerala which have altitude of 1,600 m above sea level. Munnar also has the highest peak in South India, Anamudi, which towers over 2,695 m. This hill station was once the summer resort of the erstwhile British Government in South India. One of the major attractions was Neelakurinji flower which blues the hills once in every twelve years, will bloom next in 2030. Eravikulam National Park which is another piece of attraction is famous for its endangered inhabitant-the Nilgiri Tahr. Another prime draw for visitors is Mattupetty situated at a height of 1700 m above sea levelis also known for its storage masonry dam and the beautiful lake, which offers pleasurable boat rides, enabling one to enjoy the surrounding hills and landscape. Pallivasal, located at about 3 km from Chithirapuram in Munnar is the venue of the first hydro-electric project in Kerala. It is a place of immense scenic beauty and is often favored by visitors as a picnic spot. Munnar has a legacy of its own when it comes to the origins and evolution of tea plantations. Taking account of this legacy and to preserve and showcase some of the exquisite and interesting aspects of the genesis and growth of tea plantations in Kerala's high ranges, a museum exclusively for tea was opened some years ago by Tata Tea in Munnar.

OBJECTIVES OF THE STUDY

1. To study the impact of COVID 19 on tourism sector in India.

2. To analyze the socio-economic and environmental impact of COVID -19 on Munnar tourism.

3. To examine the programs and policy measures by the government in tourism sector.

METHODOLOGY OF THE STUDY

The study includes both primary and secondary data. The primary data is collected through random sampling which include 30 tourists and 30 tourist guides. Secondary data includes various reports from newspaper articles, journals and books.

IMPACT ON TOURISM SECTOR

In Kerala, the tourism sector rebounded strongly in 2019 after the 2018 foods and the year 2019 witnessed the highest growth rate in domestic and foreign tourist arrivals in the last 24 years. There was 8.52 per cent growth in foreign tourist arrivals and 17.81 per cent growth in domestic tourist arrivals in 2019 over 2018 in the State. The Covid-19 pandemic had hit business as well as employees of the industry on same extent. The tourism industry in the State is facing unprecedented losses due to lock down situation in the wake of Covid-19.

Table 1: Total Tourist arrivals in Kerala

Tourist arrivals	2019	2020
Domestic Tourist	1,83,84,233	49,88,972
Foreign Tourist	11,89,233	3,40,755
Earnings from Tourist arrivals (in crores)	45,019	11,336

Source: Newspaper article

The outbreak of the pandemic and lockdown that followed have been disastrous for Kerala as tourism alone contributes 10 per cent to the state's economy and employs 23.5 per cent of the total workforce. The foreign tourist arrivals in the state slumped by 72% from 11.89 lakh in 2019 to 3.40 lakh in 2020. Likewise, the domestic tourist arrivals too plunged by 71% to 53.29 lakh in 2020 from 1.9 crore in 2019. Consequently, the earnings from tourism declined by 75%. The revenue generated from tourist footfall was 11,336 crore last year as compared to 45,200 crore in 2019 (Kerala Tourism.org).

Anticipating 10 per cent growth over 2019, the number of foreign tourists' arrivals estimated for the period from January 2020 to September 2020 was 9,01, 971. Similarly, assuming a 20 per cent growth in domestic tourist arrivals, the projected number of tourist arrivals between January to September, 2020 was 1,58,21,071. However, the estimated number of domestic tourists in this period is only 39,31,591. The decline in numbers is almost 75 per cent. The total loss in the sector from January to September 2020 is 24971 crore. Out of this 20,303 is loss in direct earnings and 4,668 is loss in indirect earnings. The loss in earnings from decline in foreign tourist arrivals is estimated to be 5, 274 crore and from domestic tourist arrivals is 19, 697 crores.

The number of foreign tourist arrivals and domestic tourist arrivals in the State from January to September in 2019 was 8,19,975 and 1,31,84,227 respectively. However, the estimated figures of tourist arrivals, foreign and domestic, in these months in 2020 are 3,49,575 and 39,31,591 respectively. The decline in arrivals as compared to 2019 is 57 per cent in foreign tourists and 70 per cent in domestic tourists. The total loss in the sector from January to September 2020 is 20,115 crore. Out of this, 16,178 crore are losses in direct earnings and 3,937 crore are losses in indirect earnings. The loss in earnings from decline in foreign tourist arrivals is 4,403 crore and from domestic tourist arrivals is 15, 712 crores. The loss in earnings in tourism is in the range of 20,000 crore to 25,000 crore over the nine months of 2020.

SOCIO ECONOMIC IMPACT OF COVID 19 ON TOURISM

As the pandemic hit the tourism sector, there had a huge impact on every spheres. Foreign tourists as well as Domestic tourist had faced a large restriction in travelling and access to other services. The cost of travelling had increased double times within a short span of time as the intensity of Covid cases had increased. The largely affected sessions were the daily wages workers, hotel workers, taxi and auto drivers, restaurant owners and tourist guides/ assistant. This study focused the socio-economic impact on tourist guides.From the data collected out of 30 tourist assistant,60% of the tourist assistant are from Tamil Nadu followed by Kerala and Karnataka. This clearly shows the dependence of migrant workers in this sector.

Table 2: State of Domicile of Tourist assistants (%)

States	Percentage of workers
Kerala	22
Tamil Nadu	60
Karnataka	10
Andra Pradesh	3.3
Others	4.7
Total	100

Source: Primary Data

Table 3: Comparative levels of income of tourist assistant

Level of income (per month)	2019(%)	2021(%)
0-5000	6.6	33.3
10000-20000	13.3	50
20000-30000	16.8	6.7
30000 and above	63.3	10
Total	100	100

Source: Primary data

There is a drastic change in the level of income of the tourist related workers due to the pandemic. On before the pandemic 63.3 percent enjoys and income of 30000 and above but after the pandemic, there is only 10 percent of the tourist assistant have the same level of income as before. The major reason behind this is due to the larger reduction in the global tourist visiting in this area.

Migrant workers are especially vulnerable to the devastating impacts of the COVID-19 pandemic. In the short-term, the crisis has left many migrant workers both unable to access their workplaces (placed under lockdown) in countries of destination and unable to return to their places of origin because of travel bans. Most are now unable to return to their state of origin due to border closures. If they are able, some have expressed fear that returned migrant workers will place strains on already struggling economies and healthcare systems. The crisis goes beyond the individual worker; families and entire nations depend on remittances to sustain themselves. COVID-19 has greatly impacted remittance flows from migrants laid-off from tourism industry jobs, and the economies dependent on this revenue are at risk for severe recession. Due to their status, they are often ineligible for unemployment benefits or other social safety nets. As a result, many migrants are left with smaller or non-existent paychecks, reducing their ability to send money home. This effect is compounded by the lack of available services to send money home and the increased cost of doing so.

ECOLOGICAL IMPACTS

Covid 19 pandemic had worsen the rhythm of the entire world but it also had a positive impact on environment. Especially in tourism related areas, the level of environmental pollution had minimized to a greater extent. Within the tourism infrastructure, transport is considered to be the most environmentally polluting. It is responsible for about 75% of CO2 emissions in tourism.As a biodiversity hotspot, Western Ghats had a profound impact on the environment and ecology. Environmental quality in the tourism sector is directly related to the number of visitors. Munnar is very ecological sensitive region where vechicle pollution is the major contributor of the air quality deterioration. Sewage wastes from the hotels and restaurants is adversely impacting the river quality and aquatic life. Slid wastes including plastics were a threat to the biodiversity itself.

 The ecological impact of the accommodation sector, or accommodation-related activities more broadly, is likely to go unnoticed due to difficulties with the carbon reporting mechanism of this economic activity. Tourism accommodation is responsible for 21% of the CO2 emissions delivered by the entire tourism industry, and the environmental impact is through greenhouse gas emissions, wastewater discharge and other. Tourism accommodation contributes significant amounts of energy consumption (mainly through the use of air conditioning, heating and lighting) and CO2. The importance of environmental orientation in tourism, including accommodation and international tourism activities, can be seen from the fact that tourism is expected to contribute about 7.5% of global CO2 emissions in 2035. However, the fact that the development of this sector of the economy may affect the reduction of emissions is confirmed by the fact that the goal of the global hotel industry is to reduce GHG emissions per room per year by 66% by 2030 and by 90% by 2050 compared to 2010 levels.(Rafał Nagaj)

With a series of lockdown and travel restrictions due to pandemic had increased the quality of environment and regain its natural freshness. It is very much visible in every tourist area. This clearly shows human interventions had impacted ecological quality deterioration.

POLICY INITIATIVES BY THE GOVERNMENT

There are various policy measures and efforts were taken to the revival of tourism section on global, national and regional levels.

> The Global Tourism Crisis Committee took an initiative to elevate and combat the effect of COVID-19 on the tourism industry in addition to its recommendations to the Ministry of Finance for providing a relief package for the tourism sector.

> · 'Dekho ApnaDesh' launched by the Ministry of Tourism is another initiative. This web-series creates awareness about tourist destinations in the country.

> Twenty-six webinars covering lesser-known tourist destinations and promoting the concept of responsible tourism were held in April 2020. Approximately 42,000 people registered for the webinars, which were well received by the travel industry, students and the public. (ministry of Tourism,2020)

> There are global forums created in order to discuss the revival strategy of tourism. The Ministry of Tourism and Government of India participated an 'Extraordinary Tourism Ministers Virtual Meeting of the G-20'. The purpose of the meeting was to facilitate collaborative action to protect tourism businesses and jobs, and support visitors in meeting the unprecedented challenge posed by COVID-19 and took suggestions on measures that could be taken to revive the confidence of the industry, consumers and stakeholders;

> The Ministry of Tourism set up a portal 'Stranded in India' aiming to facilitate and extend support to foreign tourists who were stranded because of the cancellation of flights and the lockdown.

> The Ministry of Tourism circulated and disseminated information on all travel-related advice and guidelines, issued by the Ministry of Health and Family Welfare and other Ministries/Organizations.

> The Government of kerala had initiated a new drive "safe Kerala and safe tourism' , to bring back visitorsto kerala to regain the sector.

> Govt of Kerala had also initiated a new strategy of tourism called "caravan tourism" as measure of responsive tourism and as per the changing needs of the visitors.

FINDINGS OF THE STUDY

The major findings of the study were,

> COVID 19 had impacted tourism sector on a large scale.70% of the

employees and tourist guides who lost their job during the pandemic period.

➤ Lack of infrastructal facility is one of the main hurdle that lags tourism in kerla.

➤ Inadequate measure to reduce ecological impacts and solid waste managements is a bigger issue that degrades the quality of kerala tourism.

➤ There is also need to update the exisiting policies on migrant labourers in this sector. They were excluded from the radius of social security nets.

➤ Covid 19 pandemic had shown as the necessity of alternate tourism sieves and innovative measures to improve the sector.

BIBLIOGRAPHY

➤ *ECONOMIC REVIEW 2020.* Thiruvananthapuram: Kerala State Planning Board, 2021.

➤ *India Brand Equity Foundation.* 3 december 2021. 8 december 2021. <https://www.ibef.org/industry/indian-tourism-and-hospitality-industry-analysis-presentation>.

➤ The New Indian Express,12.05.2020.

➤ *KERALA DEVELOPMENT REPORT: INITIATIVES,AND CHALLENGES.* govt report. Thiruvananthapuram: Kerala State Planning Board, 2021.

➤ *Kerala Tourism.org.* n.d. 12 12 2021. <https://www.keralatourism.org/>.

➤ "ministry of Tourism,2020." n.d.

➤ Rafał Nagaj, Brigita Žuromskaite˙. "Tourism in the Era of Covid-19 and Its Impact on the environment." *Energies* (2021).

➤ Sigala, Marianna. "Tourism and COVID-19: Impacts and implications for advancing and resetting industry and research." *Elsevier Public Health Emergency Collection* (2020): 312-321.

➤ Siby, K. M, and others, "The Economic Impact Of Covid-19 Pandemic On The Travel And Tourism Industry: Kerala Evidence," MPRA Paper 108242, University Library of Munich, Germany, 2021.

➤ *UNWTO.* n.d. 10 December 2021. <https://www.unwto.org/tourism-and-covid-19-unprecedented-economic-impacts>.

➤ Helen Dempster and Cassandra Zimmer,Migrant Workers in the Tourism Industry: How Has COVID-19 Affected Them, and What Does the Future Hold?(2020)

CHAPTER 5

AN ANALYSIS ON THE IMPACT OF COVID-19 ON THE TOURISM SECTOR IN KERALA ECONOMY

Dr. Vineeth Mathew
Assistant Professor,
Holy Cross College, Kozhikode

ABSTRACT

World has been facing a rare pandemic of COVID19 since December 2019. Most of the countries in the World had affected seriously and implemented the lock down and social distancing practices to overcome the pandemic situation. The pandemic has created a multiple crisis in the world economy in the various sectors such as health, travel and tourism, education, finance, GDP, employment, prices, emigration and remittances, economic situation of governments etc. In India, the different stages of lockdown has created heavy damage on all sectors of national and state's economy and drive the economy to a unusual recession. Kerala economy was also greatly affected by the pandemic in all the spheres. Kerala tourism has been a significant contributor to the economy of Kerala over the decades and the sector has been the worst hit and facing unexpected challenge by the pandemic which brought the entire industry in to stagnation. Therefore, this paper aims to analyse the impact of Covid-19 on the Kerala tourism industry.

Key words – Covid-19, Pandemic, Tourism, Economic impact

INTRODUCTION

Covid-19 pandemic is an extraordinary situation for the entire world, which has potentially damaged almost all sectors of life. Due this pandemic crisis, the tourism and hospitality sector has collapsed in almost all parts of the world and the same for India and Kerala. Tourism, the vibrant and dynamic sector, continues to play significant role in Kerala economy by making visible contribution to employment, income and foreign exchange earnings. The pandemic broke out when the travel and tourism industry was at its peak. The spread of the pandemic was very fast and forced the country into a complete lockdown and thereby great slowdown in every sectors of the economy.

The lockdown has shaken the Kerala economy entirely by hitting different economic sectors, mainly in the tourism industry, which is one of the main contributors to State Domestic Product. The national lockdown implemented due to the pandemic has directly affected the various transport sectors such as aviation, railways and other which have a significant impact on the tourism industry. As the travels are restricted, this brings about a great reduction of activities in all dimensions of the economy. Due to the unexpected tragic situations arise of Covid 19, all the areas of the tourism industry move to a stage of stagnation and results the downfall of the entire tourism sector in the state.

OBJECTIVE OF THE PAPER

The main objective of the paper is to analyse the economic impact of covid-19 on the tourism sector of Kerala.

METHODOLOGY

Only secondary data have been used for the analysis and description of the objective. It was collected and combined from different books, research papers, reports, journals, online data base which are related to Covid -19 pandemic.

KERALA ECONOMY AND TOURISM SECTOR IN THE PRE-POST COVID SITUATION

During the past two decades, Kerala had shown significant growth in the tourism sector even as industry and others lagged. In 2018-19, the state reported the highest growth rate in domestic and foreign tourist arrivals in the last 24 years and there was around 8.5 per cent growth in foreign and 17.8 per cent growth in domestic tourist arrivals in 2019 compared to 2018. But the covid -19 pandemic taken all our gains. Tourism is an important contributor to the service sector in Kerala. The total revenue generated from tourism during the year 2015-16 was around 26,689.63 crores which shows an increase of 7.25 per cent in 2014-15.

During the last decade, the total revenue earned from tourism sector registered a growth rate of 11.33 per cent. It grew from 7,738 crores in 2005-06-16 to 26,689.63 crores by 2015. Between 2013 and 2015, a declining tendency of the growth rate was noticed from 12.22 per cent in 2013 to 7.25 per cent by 2015.

The contribution of tourism sector to total employment in Kerala has several impacts like direct, indirect and induced impacts. Employment opportunities generated by tourism in the Kerala economy are directly in the areas like travel agencies, hotel sector and airlines and indirectly to retail, construction, manufacturing and telecommunications.

CONTRIBUTION OF TOURISM SECTOR TO TOTAL EMPLOYMENT

Share in Employment (in per cent)			
Country/ State	Direct share	Indirect + Induced share	Total share
India	4.4	5.8	10.2
Kerala	9.9	13.6	23.5

The COVID-19 pandemic has shattered Kerala's tourism industry. The tourism sector alone employs about 15 lakh people and contributes 11.5 per cent of the state's GDP. From the hill stations of Munnar and Wayanad to the backwaters of Alappuzha, tourism in Kerala has taken a severe hit due to the pandemic.

According to State Tourism data, domestic arrivals fell by 72.86 per cent in 2020-21 from the year 2019-20, and international arrivals have also reduced significantly by 71.36 per cent. The first three months of this year, before fears of the third wave loomed over, the state recorded a 40.53 per cent decline in domestic and 95.65 per cent decline in international arrivals compared to the same period last year 2019-2020.The total earnings of the sector, which in 2019-20, stood at Rs 45,010 crore is now only Rs 11,000 in 2020-21.

CONCLUSION

The tourism sector has been the worst hit and the state government has announced a package to revive the industry, focusing more on domestic travellers. All round planning is needed for the development of tourism because it is a promising potential of the state. To make Kerala as an all-time tourism destination, new destinations should be adopted. Kerala is a state where 'the season never ends, hence a coordination among various departments is needed for the revamp of the sector.

REFERENCES

- www.keralatourism.gov.in

- Kerala Development Report, 2019–20

- Impact of the Covid-19 Pandemic and Lockdown on Kerala Economy, State Planning Board

- Impact of the Covid-19 on Kerala Economy - B A Prakash

- Economic Review-Kerala State Planning Board.

- Kerala Tourism Statistics, 2019

- An Analysis of Recent Trends in Kerala tourism, IOSR Journal Of Humanities And Social Science (IOSR-JHSS) Volume 24, Issue 10, Series. 4 (October. 2019) 01-15

CHAPTER 6

TOURISM SECTOR IN THE AFTERMATH OF CORONA IN KERALA

Dr. Geetha Lakshmi
Bishop Abraham Memorial College,
Thuruthicadu

ABSTRACT

Kerala, the greenest state, is on the southernmost tip of India is blessed with excellent tropical weather and networked by 44 rivers, 34 lakes, canals, ponds, paddy fields that have made it popularly known as the 'Gods Own Country" in the tourism circles. This lush green strip of land lying between the Arabian Sea and the steep Western Ghats has an area of about 38,863sq.km and is inhabited by about 33.39 million people as per Census – 2011.

The new tourism minister realises that during the past 24 years, God's own Country had shown significant growth in the tourism sector even as industry and others lagged. The two consecutive floods in 2018 and 2019, and now the Covid-19 pandemic, compressed the tourism sector. After the 2018 mega floods, the state reported the highest growth rate in domestic and foreign tourist arrivals in the last 24 years. There was around 8.5 per cent growth in foreign and 17.8 per cent growth in domestic tourist arrivals in 2019 compared to 2018. The global promotional campaigns, novel initiatives like introducing new destinations to international bloggers and developing event destinations helped the state to achieve this unique growth. With the pandemic, we have lost all our gains. This paper discusses the impact of Corona Virus on Kerala tourism, by using secondary data.

Keywords: Tourism, Foreign Tourist, Domestic Tourist, Eco- Friendly, Ecology, Backwaters and vicious circles.

INTRODUCTION

Kerala is popularly known as 'Gods Own Country' in the tourism circles. It is one of the most popular tourist destinations in the country , named as one of the ten paradises of the world by National Geographic Traveler.

Kerala is famous especially for its eco-friendly destinations in India, The land of coconuts, beautiful backwaters, beautiful beaches, rich culture, sumptuous food, natural diversity, ancient temple and blessed with excellent tropical weather and networked by 44 rivers, 34 lakes, canals, ponds, and paddy fields, is now at the first spot in the top 20 global trending destinations for 2020, as per a survey by a popular online marketplace for travellers. Kerala is already favored by many tourists from India and abroad due to its natural diversity. Growing at a rate of 13.31%, the touris industry is a major contributor to the state's economy.

The main tourism agenda for the state is promoting ecologically sustained tourism, which focuses on the local culture, wilderness adventures, volunteering and personal growth of the local population. Efforts are taken to minimize the adverse effects of traditional tourism on the natural environment, and enhance the cultural integrity of local people.

The rapid outbreak of corona virus (COVID-19) not only affected the global economy on a massive scale but also challenged human life. The rapid spread of the virus modified normal economic activities and pushed some production centres into vicious circles. As per the World Health Organization's (WHO) dashboard report, this dangerous virus pandemic has resulted in over 4.3 million confirmed cases and over 549,000 deaths (9 July 2020). In the case of India, tourism is one of the evergreen industries, contributing 9.3% to GDP in 2018; this is expected to increase to around 10% in 2028 (WTTC, 2020). Therefore, the impact of Covid has been very high on our tourism industry especially in Kerala.

KERALA TOURIST STATISTICS 2018

Kerala is well known for its beaches, backwaters in Alappuzha and Kollam, mountain ranges and wildlife sanctuaries. Other popular attractions in the state include

➤ The beaches at Kovalam, Varkala, Kollam and Kappad;

➤ Backwater tourism and lake resorts around Ashtamudi Lake, Kollam; Hill stations and resorts at Munnar, Wayanad, Nelliampathi, Vagamon and Ponmudi;

➤ National parks and wildlife sanctuaries at Periyar, Parambikulam and Eravikulam.

➤ The Heritage sites, such as the Padmanabhapuram Palace, Hill Palace, and Mattancherry Palace.

➤ To further promote tourism in Kerala, the Grand Kerala Shopping Festival was started by the Government of Kerala in 2007. Since then it has been held every year during the December–January period.

Kerala is an established destination for both domestic as well as foreign tourists. Kerala is a leader in India when it comes to destination management, tourism promotion as well as tourist arrivals. The statistics are as shown below:

Foreign Tourists

Foreign tourists are people visiting India on a foreign passport. They stay at least twenty four hours in the country. The purpose of their journey can be classified as follows.

1. Leisure

2. Business

The following are not regarded as 'foreign tourists'

(i) Persons arriving with or without a contract, to take up an occupation or engage in activities. They receive remuneration from within the country

(ii) Persons coming to live in the country

(iii) Temporary visitors staying less than twenty four hours in the country.

Domestic Tourists

Domestic tourists are people who travel within the country to a place other than their usual place of residence .They stays at hotels or other accommodation establishments run on commercial basis for a duration of not less than 24 hours or one night .Their purpose of travel may be classified as

i) Pleasure

ii)Religious pilgrimage

iii) Business

iv) Study

v) Health

Total number of Tourists – Before CORONA

The following table gives the data on foreign and Domestic Tourist arrival for years. From 2015 onwards, it can be seen that there is a steady increase in Tourist arrival. The table shows the increasing trend in tourist inflow Kerala from 2015 to 2019.

Table No: 1; Tourist Arrivals 2015 – 2019

Tourist Arrival	2015	2016	2017	2018	2019
Tourists (Foreign & Domestic)	13443050	14210954	15765390	16701068	19574004
Percentage of variation over previous year	6.73	5.71	10.94	5.94	17.2

Source: India Tourism official website, India Tourism Statistics 2019

EARNINGS FROM TOURISM IN KERALA

Foreign exchange earnings from tourism have shown a steady growth over the years. In 2019, Kerala has earned Rs.10271.06 crores as foreign exchange earnings from tourism against Rs.8764.46 crores in the year 2018 showing a growth of 17.19 %. Table No:2 shows the estimates of earnings from foreign tourists for the last five years.

Table No: 2; Earnings From Tourism, 2015-2019 (Rs. in Crores)

Year	Foreign Exchange Earnings	% of Increase	Earnings from Domestic Tourists	Total revenue generated from Tourism(Direct & Indirect)	% of Increase
2015	6949.88	8.61	13836.78	26689.63	7.25
2016	7749.51	11.51	15348.64	29658.56	11.12
2017	8392.11	8.29	17608.22	33383.68	12.56
2018	8764.46	4.44	19474.62	36258.01	8.61
2019	10271.06	17.19	24785.62	45010.69	24.14

*Source – Kerala Tourism official website, Kerala Tourism Statistics 2019

TOTAL NUMBER OF TOURISTS – AFTER CORONA

Around 18.4 million domestic and 1.18 million foreign tourists visited Kerala in 2019. Since the state reported its first Covid positive case on January 2020, only 349,575 foreign tourists visited in the year, a 61 per cent decline in numbers compared to the previous year. Domestic tourist arrivals also drastically declined by 85%, resulting in total losses of Rs 35,207 crore in 2020. Around 7,022 accommodation units with 88,733 rooms (including home stays) are available in the state; Alappuzha leads with the highest number of accommodation units, 173, while Kasargod has the lowest, 85 units.

IMPACT OF CORONA ON KERALA TOURISM

➤ The tourism industry contributes 12 percent to the state's GDP. Hotels, restaurants and resorts wear a deserted look due to the pandemic. Having already incurred huge losses, hoteliers don't expect the industry to revive anytime soon.The hotel industry is struggling to meet the expenses, with the tourist inflow dipping sharply. The hotels witnessed a rush of local visitors when restrictions were eased after September last year. But it was hardly sufficient to run the property.

➤ In the absence of tourists from other states or from outside the country, these boats are now mostly plying local visitors at discounted rates for a few hours. Houseboats have only local visitors. Houseboat owners are grappling with another problem: cost of fuel.

➤ Domestic tourists have become the mainstay of Kerala tourism since the state was hit by one of the worst floods of the century and Nipah virus contagion in 2018. But the subsequent year saw a healthy increase in tourist inflow. Domestic travellers accounted for 94 percent of the 1.96 crore visitors to the state in 2019, showing a rise of 18 percent over the previous year.

➤ Weddings, conferences and other occasions cancelled or postponed, that created a huge revenue loss.

➤ Kerala has been well known for hundreds of years for its practice of Ayurveda. In Kerala Ayurveda is not just a healthcare system but it is a part and parcel of every aspect of life, in fact it is a lifestyle in Kerala so to speak. Travellers from the western world have been travelling here for spiritual and physical awakenings ever since the Beatles made their sojourn to India in the mid-1960s. Ayurveda is popular in UK, France, Spain, Italy, Germany and few Gulf countries like Saudi Arabia and UAE. The growth rate of tourists flocking for Ayurveda is increasing every year. The functioning of Ayurveda resorts has stopped due to Corona.

➤ COVID-19 not only affected the tourism industry as a whole but the penetration of effects is severe in ancillary industries such as hotels, restaurants, markets in tourist areas and travel industries. Ultimately, there has been a downturn trend of GDP, and the lives of people have been put in doubt.

The world is still coming to terms with the COVID-19 outbreak, especially towards the containment of collateral damage in different sectors of the economy. The impact been clearly seen: there is no production, distribution and mobility of people for economic activities as there is partial or complete shutdown in most parts of the world. The COVID-19 pandemic has damaged the channels of sustainable development, particularly in countries striving for substantial economic growth through the development of tourism. At the same time, the luxury hotels, airlines and shipping companies are in a critical situation as a result of the COVID-19 pandemic. Therefore, it can be revealed that the Corona virus pandemic has not only taken thousands of lives but also made the tourism industry in this region vulnerable.

GOVERNMENT INITIATIVES

The Global Tourism Crisis Committee related to COVID-19 held its third virtual meeting on 16 April 2020. The meeting was chaired by the Secretary General UNWTO and included high level representatives from both public and private sectors, and international organisations such as WHO, International Civil Aviation Organization (ICAO), IATA, WT TC. The Secretary of Tourism highlighted the efforts made by the Ministry of Tourism, Government of India to combat the crisis.

During the meeting, the participants were informed about the initiatives undertaken by UNWTO and other tourism stakeholders to meet the challenge posed by COVID-19. The following is a list of the Indian Ministry of Tourism initiatives conducted to elevate and combat the effect of COVID-19 on the tourism industry in addition to its recommendations to the Ministry of Finance for providing a relief package for the tourism sector:

The Ministry of Tourism launched the 'Dekho ApnaDesh' web-series with a view to create awareness about tourist destinations in the country. Twenty-six webinars covering lesser-known tourist destinations and promoting the concept of responsible tourism were held in April 2020. Approximately 42,000 people registered for the webinars, which were well received by the travel industry, students and the public (Ministry of Tourism, 2020);

An 'Extraordinary Tourism Ministers Virtual Meeting of the G-20' chaired by H.E. Minister of Tourism, Kingdom of Saudi Arabia was held on 24 April 2020. The purpose of the meeting was to facilitate collaborative action to protect tourism businesses and jobs, and support visitors in meeting the unprecedented challenge posed by COVID-19. The Ministry of Tourism and Government of India participated and took suggestions on measures that could be taken to revive the confidence of the industry, consumers and stakeholders;

The Ministry of Tourism set up a portal 'Stranded in India' aiming to facilitate and extend support to foreign tourists who were stranded because of the cancellation of flights and the lockdown. The site also provided Helpline numbers of the Ministry of Health & Family Welfare, Bureau of Immigration, Ministry of Tourism, and Ministry of External Affairs. A total of 2,142 foreign tourists have sought assistance through the portal up to 30 April 2020;

The Ministry of Tourism circulated and disseminated information on all travel-related advice and guidelines, issued by the Ministry of Health and Family Welfare and other Ministries/Organizations. This related to various steps to be taken by tourists, hotels and other stakeholders in all travel and hospitality associations;

Hotel associations were advised not to deny accommodation to foreign tourists and to follow required procedures prescribed by the Ministry of Health and Family Welfare. OYO Hotels collaborated by opening up their accommodation units across the country for stranded tourists. This information was shared with States/ UTs, Embassies and others in order to utilise the accommodation units for tourists;

The Minister of State for Tourism and Culture launched the Incredible India Website in Chinese, Arabic and Spanish to attract tourists from these regions. The function was attended by senior officials of the Ministry, foreign delegates and stakeholders of the tourism industry.

FINDINGS OF THE STUDY

Tourism is an important source of generation of income. So every country should take the responsibility to promote tourism. Here I am discussing about conditions to improve the facilities for tourists

1. Foreign tourists are very particular hygiene. So the authorities should give more importance to their safety and hygiene.

2. Another difficulty faced by them are the presence of middlemen, who are present at all levels. This menace is getting worse by the day. Demands have been made to control and keep a watch over such people.

3. Majority of them are preferring homely stay. Government officials give guidelines regarding the functioning of home stays are issued regularly and inspections are also conducted alongside.

OTHER FINDINGS ARE

1. During 2019 the maximum number of foreign tourists arrived in January followed by December. The maximum number of foreign tourists arrived during the 1st quarter of the year 2019, constituting 35.51 % with 422469 tourists followed by 4th quarter constituting 31.08 % with 369796tourists, the 3rd quarter constituting 18.09% with 215186 tourists and the 2nd quarter constituting 15.32% with 182320 tourists.

2. During 2019, the maximum number of domestic tourists arrived during the 4th quarter constituting 28.29% with 5200006 tourists followed by 2nd quarter constituting 25.97 % with 4773739 tourists, the 3rd quarter constituting 22.95% with 4220020 tourists and the 1st quarter constituting 22.79 % with 4190468 tourists.

3. Kerala Tourism Minister said a rejuvenation package for tourism in the state has been prepared and will be implemented to attract tourists to the state after the COVID-19 crisis is over.

4. The state's tourism sector has incurred a loss of 15,000 crore due to the corona virus-induced lockdown.

CONCLUSION OF THE STUDY

Kerala is one of the best tourist centers in India and many foreigners visit our country especially Kerala. Kerala is famous for its backwaters and forty four rivers. Compared with other states , Kerala is having the facility of boating especially in Kuttanad. Kuttanad is famous for its scenic beauty. The place is almost covered with water throughout the year as it is a low lying area when compared with other regions. The tourist can enjoy different varieties of food items especially coconut toddy, varieties of fish and other sea food items obtained from the lakes. Such food items are not available fresh in other parts of the country. Tourist can have an entirely different eco system, climatic conditions and they can even live in water for weeks in the rented house boats.

The impact of Covid has been very high on our tourism industry in Kerala. The spread of the pandemic was so fast and gripping that the country itself got into complete lockdown and consequent shocks in every aspect of the economy. The study attempted to analyze the changes that occurred in the tourism industry in Kerala as a result of the pandemic. The study inferred from the analysis that lockdowns due to the Covid pandemic had significant and enduring negative impacts on the business prospects of stakeholders in the tourism industry in Kerala.

REFERENCES

Websites

- Accreditation Of Hospitals To Promote Top Medical Tourism Destination In India Archived 26 September 2007 at the Way back Machine
- "Best Beaches of Kerala". *irisholidays.com. 14 February 2015.*
- Importance of Kuttanad, 7 February 2018, ENVIS Centre: Kerala State of Environment and Related Issues, Hosted by Kerala State Council for Science, Technology and Environment, Sponsored by Ministry of Environment, Forests & Climate Change, Government of India.
- Lisha Anna, Will Kerala witness a new tourism culture post-Covid? September 27, 2021; https://www.onmanorama.com/travel/kerala/2021/09/27/will-kerala-witness-new-tourism-culture-post-covid.html
- shodhganga.inflibnet.ac.in/bitstream/10603/19587/17/17_conclusion.pdf
- The New Indian Express,12.05.2020.
- The Indian Express. 24,12,2021.
- http://www.keralatourism.org/ destination wise foreign, 2010
- "7 Best Kerala Backwaters You Should Explore- Travel News India".

Reports

- Kerala Sastra Sahitya Parishad, Report of the study team on Kuttanad, Sarada Printing Press, Trivandram. (1978).

- The Report of the Expert Committee on Paddy Cultivation, Main Report, Thiruvananthapuram(1999) vol.1.

- "Kerala Tourism – Super brand". *Super brand status of Kerala Tourism brand. Government of Kerala. Archived from* the original *on 12 July 2006.* Retrieved 9 August *2006.*

- "Tourist statistics – 2008" (PDF). *Government of Kerala, Tourism Department.* Retrieved 22 October *2010.*

- India Water Portal, October 2011, Pollution of the Pampa River, a major environmental issue for the Central Travancore and Kuttanad regions of Kerala, *Monday, 18 July 2011 at 1745 hrs IST (18 July 2011).*

- "Andhra Pradesh top tourist destination: Tourism Ministry". *Financialexpress.com. Archived from* the original *on 21 February 2014.* Retrieved 13 August *2012.*

- Kerala Tourism, Statistics 2018, Research and Statistics Division Department of Tourism, 2018.

- *Ministry of Tourism ,Government of India, Tourism Statistics at a Glance- 2019.*

Books and Journals

- Abdul Jamal, A. Sankaran, Yasmeen Sultana, Effect and Impact of the Corona virus Pandemic (COVID-19) on Tourism Industry in India: A review, In book: CORONAVIRUS: the management of pandemic and the impact on Agenda 2030 (pp.171-187), September 2020.

- *Cuskelly, Claudia,*"New era in Indian getaways: Recharge your batteries with this safe-haven holiday to Kerala". *Express.co.uk.* Retrieved 14 August *2019.*

- "Directorate General of Lighthouses and Lightships". *DGLL.* Retrieved 31 August *2015.*

- Edayady A. C. Mathew, Ormachakrangal (Malayalam), ACM Publications,2002.

- Geetha Lakshmi, Agricultural Development and Ecological Imbalance in Kuttanad, *International Journal of Social Science and Economic Research,* ISSN: 2455-8834,Volume:03, Issue:12 "December 2018"

- Jeemon Jacob, Covid-19: Kerala tourism sector hit hard by the pandemic, India Today, June 9, 2021.

- "Kerala tourism commercial gets award". *Archived from* the original *on 5 October 2009.*

- Nelliyat Prakash, Tuesday, The Hindu, News Paper, 2018 May 1.

- Padmakumar, K.G.,Rice-Fish Rotation: A Sustainable Farming Model For Coastal Lowlands K.G. Padmakumar, regional Agricultural Research Station, Kumarakom

- 686 566. Edited by Dr. Vandana Shiva and Dr. Poonam Pandey, Biodiversity Based Organic Farming, A New Paradigm for Food Security and Food Safety, Navdanya, New Delhi, 2006.

➤ Prakash, Pillai R, Research Report, Labour Movements in Agriculture Sector: A Case Study of Kuttanad Region. Kerala Institute of Labour and Employment, Thiruvananthapuram, Loyola College of Social Sciences, Sreekariyam, Thiruvananthapuram -695 017, (2015).

➤ Siby, K. M, and others, "The Economic Impact Of Covid-19 Pandemic On The Travel And Tourism Industry: Kerala Evidence," MPRA Paper 108242, University Library of Munich, Germany, 2021.

CHAPTER 7

CONSEQUENCES OF CORONA ON THE TOURISM SECTOR IN KERALA

Divya Kochukoshy
Assistant Professor
Bishop Abraham Memorial College,
Thuruthicadu

ABSTRACT

The current COVID-19 pandemic is leading to significant changes in terms of people's economic behavior, which will inevitably impact the tourism industry and tourism activity both worldwide and in tourism host countries. Immediate control measures, such as necessary restrictions on travel, avoiding physical contact, social distancing, as well as tourists' and patients' changes in priority making, have vanished interest in traveling away from the place of usual residence and seeking to receive tourism services. COVID-19 pandemic has caused immediate impacts across the whole spectrum of economic and social activity. The duration and intensity of the arising malfunction in tourism are not yet known; thus, it is too early to make any assessments of the financial losses that will be recorded on an annual basis. However, an initial approach is necessary in order to assess the range of to date impacts, aiming at a critical appraisal of the current situation. It will mainly help in making the appropriate pandemic management plan in the tourism industry.

Over 10 million foreign tourist arrived in India in 2017 compared to 8.89 million in 2016 representing of growth of 15.6% domestic tourist visit to all states and union territories numbered 1,036.35 million in 2012. In 2018, 17.42 million foreign tourist arrived in India. In 2020, approximately 6.33 million international tourists and non resident Indians arrived in India, down from about 18 million in 2019. Tourist Arrivals in India increased to 29397 in June from 13307 in May of 2021.

Aviation and Tourism It is the first and foremost severely hit industries. India has the fourth largest aviation market in the world and is going through major losses internationally. The only way of recovery is via domestic flights operation if the pandemic is controlled. According to the International Airport Transport Association, it is estimated that there is a loss of USD 252 billion to the industry and travel sector has shrunk up by 25% in 2020. This has resulted in a loss of 50 million jobs. In India, the potential job loss is around 38 million which is about 70% of total workforce.

Keywords: COVID-19, Pandemic.

INTRODUCTION

Tourism has become one of the largest and rapidly growing sectors of the world economy. It is projected as a very valuable one for the overall development of a country and particularly for the fast development of the developing countries. Tourism does not have a unique base as an industry, but encompasses widely disparate firms and organizations from many industries, which serve with a variety of incomes, tastes and objectives. Tourism is the travel for predominantly recreational or leisure purposes or the provisional services to support this leisure travel. The world Tourism Day is celebrated on September 27.

CORONA is the greatest emergency for the world in last 75 years especially, after the World War II. The Corona virus or COVID-19 pandemic is massively affecting Kerala's tourism industry. Even the famous tourist spot of Kovalam beach, which is usually swarmed with tourists, was seen deserted on Sunday. Kerala has so far reported 22 confirmed cases of COVID-19.

SIGNIFICANCE OF TOURISM

Tourism is an important, even vital, source of income for many regions and countries. Its importance was recognized in the Manila Declaration on World Tourism of 1980 as an"an activity essential to the life of nations because of its direct effects on the social, cultural, educational, and economic sectors of national societies and on their international relations.

Tourism brings in large amounts of income into a local economy in the form of payment for goods and services needed by tourists, accounting for 30% of the world's trade of services, and 6% of overall exports of goods and services. It also creates opportunity for employment in the service sector of the economy associated with tourism.

The service industries which benefit from tourism include transportation services, such as airlines, cruise ships, and taxicabs; hospitality services, such as accommodations, including hotels and resorts; and entertainment venues, such as amusement parks, casinos, shopping malls, music venues, and theatres. This is in addition to goods bought by tourists, including souvenirs.

DEFINITION

In 1936 the League of Nations defined a foreign tourist as "someone travelling abroad for at least twenty-four hours". Its successor, the United Nations, amended this definition in 1945, by including a maximum stay of six month.

In 1994, the United Nations identified three forms of tourism in its Recommendations on Tourism statistics:

➤ Domestic tourism, involving residents of the given country travelling only within this country

➤ Inbound tourism, involving non-residents travelling in the given country

➤ Outbound tourism, involving residents travelling in another country.

The terms tourism and travel are sometimes used interchangeably. In this context, travel has a similar definition to tourism, but implies a more purposeful journey. The terms tourism and tourist are sometimes used pejoratively, to imply a shallow interest in the cultures or locations visited. By contrast, traveler is often used as a sign of distinction. The sociology of tourism has studied the cultural values underpinning these distinctions and their implications for class relations.

TOURISM: INDIAN SCENARIO

Tourism is a significant part of India's service economy. The National Tourism Policy of 1982 gave a new ethos and values to tourism in its purpose, direction and development. It aims "to promote tourism as a means to ensure a more meaningful and wider understanding of India and its people amongst all sections of the societies with in the country and abroad and to achieve sustained economic development and positive social change through development of tourism while preserving and protecting the environment and heritage". The Indian scenario presents some emerging trends in the tourist sector as a catalyst for its development. The contribution of tourism services in the GDP for 2009-2010 is estimated 14.36% including its direct and indirect effect. It is the third largest net earner of foreign exchange and contributes to 10% of the total employment in the Kerala tourism.

Tourism is the majority of the enjoyable and other features of travel destination and provision of facilities and services of the pleasure travelers. Tourism in India is important for the country's economy and is growing rapidly. The world travel and tourism council calculated the tourism generated. Rs 16.91 lacks crore (US$ 240 billion) or 9.2% of India GDP in 2018 and supported, 42.763 million jobs 8.1% of its employment the sector is predicted to grow at annual rate of 6.9% to 32.05 lacks crore by 2028 (9.9% GDP). In October 2015, India medical tourism sector was estimated to the worth US 3 billion. Over 10 million foreign tourist arrived in India in 2017 compared to 8.89 million in 2016 representing of growth of 15.6% domestic tourist visit to all states and union territories numbered 1,036.35 million in 2012. In 2018, 17.42 million foreign tourist arrived in India. In 2020, approximately 6.33 million international tourists and non resident Indians arrived in India, down from about 18 million in 2019. Tourist Arrivals in India increased to 29397 in June from 13307 in May of 2021.

OBJECTIVES

1. To analyze the impact of COVID 19 on tourism sector in Kerala.

2. To study the changes in tourism sector before and after COVID 19.

3. To find out the policies taken by the Government to overcome this situation.

METHODOLOGY

Secondary data were collected from different sources. The main sources of secondary data were India Tourism Statistics, Kerala Tourism Statistics, Kerala Economic Review, and Department of Tourism, journals, books, the internet and other published source.

KERALA AT A GLANCE

Kerala, the greenest state, is on the southernmost tip of India is blessed with excellent tropical weather and networked by 44 rivers, 34 lakes, canals, ponds, paddy fields that have made it popularly known as the 'Gods Own Country" in the tourism circles. This lush green strip of land lying between the Arabian Sea and the steep Western Ghats has an area of about 38,863sq.km and is inhabited by about 33.39 million people as per Census – 2011. Kerala has always been leading among the states in different human development indicators like highest literacy, life expectancy and lowest child mortality

Kerala Tourism is having a global presence and with its clear strategy for growth sheer marketing activities, it has gained a lot of tourist from all over the world, especially from UK, USA, France , Germany, Saudi Arabia and Australia. Kerala Tourism is to position itself as a global destination for tourism which is based on the advantage of the local resources, thereby attracting investment and resulting into sustainable development for the people of Kerala. An equable climate, a long shoreline with serene beaches, tranquil stretches of emerald backwaters, lush hill stations and exotic wildlife, waterfalls, sprawling plantations and paddy fields, enchanting art forms, magical festivals, historic and cultural monuments, exotic cuisine, all of which makes Kerala a unique experience.

Kerala has been well known for hundreds of years for its practice of Ayurveda. Ayurveda is the traditional health science of India. The word "Ayurveda" means science of life which explains the knowledge of various guidelines to be followed to keep one healthy. In Kerala Ayurveda is not just a healthcare system but it is a part and parcel of every aspect of life, in fact it is a lifestyle in Kerala so to speak. The growth rate of tourists flocking for Ayurveda is increasing every year.

The backwater of Kerala is a unique product of state and is found nowhere else in the world. Backwaters are a network of lakes, canals and estuaries and deltas of forty-four rivers that drain into the Arabian Sea. The backwaters of Kerala are a self-supporting eco-system teeming with aquatic life. The canals connect the villages together and are still used for local transport. The Kerala Backwaters offer a spectacular opportunity to see Kerala and are easily traversed by boat. Houseboat rentals are very popular with honeymooners.

The downturn has hit all categories of the hospitality industry, including hotels of the Kerala Tourism Development Corporation (KTDC), home stays, and MICE (Meeting, Incentive, Convention,Exhibition). Even prime properties of the KTDC, such as Tea County and Bolghatty, have been hit, with the dip in occupancy during the January 15-February period hovering at 25 to 30%. However, Samudra property in Kovalam has bucked the trend.

KERALA'S TOURISM ASSETS – CATEGORIZATION

The various tourist attractions in Kerala can be classified broadly as cultural attractions and natural attractions. In the listing that follows, most of the tourism assets have been assigned letter codes in the margin, based on the principal interests that they cater to. The coding pattern is given below.

Cultural Attractions	Natural Attractions
• History, architecture, • archeology • Culture, heritage, arts & crafts • Museum, palace • Fort • Religious place, pilgrimage centre, place of worship	• Beach • Backwater • Picnic spot • Hill station, hill, mountain peak • Wildlife/bird sanctuary, forest • Waterfalls • Lake

Source: Kerala Tourist Statistics, 2019

IMPACT OF CORONA ON TOURISM SECTOR IN KERALA

The crisis is an opportunity to rethink how tourism interacts with our societies, other economic sectors and our natural resources and ecosystems; to measure and manage it better; to ensure a fair distribution of its benefits and to advance the transition towards a carbon neutral and resilient tourism economy.

Hotel Business

The pandemic has severely dented the hotel business in Kerala. This business that thrived on feeding hundreds of people daily is now going through tough times. Most of the hotels had to shut down during the lockdown. Though some of the restaurants were allowed to function with only takeaway and home delivery services. Around 3000 hotels and their staff are still struggling to make ends meet.

Employment

The COVID-19 pandemic has had a significant effect on labour market for every state. 15.56 lakh Keralites returned to the state from abroad after the outbreak of Covid 19, and of this, more than 71 % had lost their jobs, as per the data of the non- resident Keralites department. Major companies in India have temporarily recessed operations in a number of manufacturing hubs and plants across the country, all of this would result in declining production and slashes of employees.

Transportation

The transport industry is the most vulnerable and effected industry during the pandemic, it is anticipated that it will be the last to recover from the impact of CORONA. The recovery of transportation is fully dependent on to what extent safety procedures were applied during the first wave of the pandemic.

Backwaters Tourism

Kerala's backwaters is the most captivating attraction for the tourists in Kerala India. The palm-lined, serene backwaters were once just Kerala's trade highways. The backwaters refer to the large inland lakes of Kerala. Kerala lives along these backwaters. The backwaters & lakes of Kerala have commanded its history, shaped her present and promise a future by ethics of offering matchless beauty and outstanding experiences. The CORONA has seriously effects Kerala's backwater tourism.

Health care

In Kerala Ayurveda is not just a healthcare system but it is a part and parcel of every aspect of life, in fact it is a lifestyle in Kerala so to speak. Travelers from the western world have been travelling here for spiritual and physical awakenings ever since the Beatles made their sojourn to India in the mid-1960s. Ayurveda is popular in UK, France, Spain, Italy, Germany and few Gulf countries like Saudi Arabia and UAE. The growth rate of tourists flocking for Ayurveda is increasing every year. So this pandemic highly affected this area.

CHANGES IN TOURISM SECTOR BEFORE AND AFTER CORONA

Kerala is a leader in India when it comes to the destination management, tourism promotion as well as tourist arrivals. The statistics are as shown below

KERALA TOURISM BEFORE CORONA

Foreign	Domestic
No. of Foreign Tourists in 2019- 1189771	No. of Domestic Tourists in 2019 - 18384233
No. of Foreign Tourists in 2018 – 1096407	No. of Domestic Tourists in 2018 - 15604661
Percentage variation over Previous year - 8.52 % Variation over Previous year - 8.52 %	Percentage Variation over Previous year - 17.81 %
Foreign Exchange Earnings 2019 - 10271.06crores	Total revenue generated 2019 - 45010.69Crores
Foreign Exchange Earnings 2018 - 8764.46crores	(Direct and Indirect)
Percentage Variation over Previous year - 17.19%	Total revenue generated
	(Direct and Indirect)2018 - 36258.01Crores
	Percentage Variation over Previous year - 24.14%

Source: Kerala Tourist Statistics, 2019

KERALA TOURISM AFTER CORONA

Around 18.4 million domestic and 1.18 million foreign tourists visited Kerala in 2019. Since the state reported its first Covid positive case on January 2020, only 349,575 foreign tourists visited in the year, a 61 per cent decline in numbers compared to the previous year. Domestic tourist arrivals also drastically declined by 85%, resulting in total losses of Rs 35,207 crore in 2020. Around 7,022 accommodation units with 88,733 rooms (including home stays) are available in the state; Alappuzha leads with the highest number of accommodation units, 173, while Kasargod has the lowest, 85 units.

PROMOTION AND PUBLICITY

The Department of Tourism has undertaken various innovative initiatives in the areas of promotion and publicity. Spice route for tourism marketing, Department of Tourism has proposed to activate the spice route destinations in Europe, Middle east and Fareast connecting muziris. The result is evident in the very high growth rate of tourist arrivals in Kerala. The major initiatives in these promotions include conducting fairs and festivals, participating in major tourism marts, advertising in print and electronic media, etc. The following are some of the International and National festivals Road shows and fairs in which the Department of Tourism has participated on 2019 -20.

SUPPORTING ORGANIZATIONS

- ➤ District Tourism Promotion Councils (DTPCs)
- ➤ Kerala Tourism Development Corporation (KTDC)
- ➤ Kerala Tourism Infrastructure Limited (KTIL)
- ➤ Kerala Institute of Tourism and Travel Studies (KITTS)
- ➤ Bekal Resort Development Corporation (BRDC)
- ➤ Muziris Heritage Projects Ltd

Kerala Adventure Tourism Promotion Society (KATPS) Kerala Adventure Tourism Promotion Society (KATPS) was registered on Oct 2012 and the mission of KATPS is to promote Kerala as an adventure tourism hub and put Kerala at the top of adventure tourism map of the county.

POLICIES TAKEN BY THE GOVERNMENT TO OVERCOME THIS SITUATION

The CORONA pandemic has the world on tenterhooks and the tourism industry has been the worst affected of all major economic sectors. Kerala's tourism sector is also facing an unprecedented crisis due to the outbreak. The Department of Tourism in Kerala is currently taking stock of the situation to devise an effective strategy to help the trade overcome the crisis.

Various departments under the Government of Kerala are putting up a united front to survive pandemic.

Post CORONA, Kerala Tourism hopes to launch short-haul tours wherein the focus will be on domestic tourism. The idea will be to promote prominent destinations in the state aggressively.

Kerala Tourism is also considering launching packages that focus on 'Learning Experiences'. This experimental model will be developed under the Responsible Tourism (RT) Mission. It will offer opportunities for travelers to learn a craft, art or martial art of Kerala by staying in the state.

1. Kerala Tourism's one-stop platform for classification/approval/ certification/accreditation of service providers. If you are a registered user, log in by entering your credentials and choose the desired service you would like to apply for.

2. Kerala Tourism opens help desks in state capital, districts

3. Kerala Tourism launches online portal for NRKs to book vehicle to return to Kerala by road.

4. Kerala Government granting various relaxations to approved hotels, resorts and home stay units in the tourism sector in view of CORONA pandemic.

5. Kerala Tourism opens help desks in state capital, districts.

6. Ministry of Tourism launches 'Stranded in India' portal to help foreign tourists stuck in various parts of India.

7. Kerala Tourism announces Working Capital Loan Scheme to support Entrepreneurs' in the Travel and Tourism Sector.

As per the Organization for Economic Cooperation and Development's (OECD) interim economic assessment, if the number of visitors would decline due to the corona virus outbreak, it would impose sizeable economic costs in OECD countries, as tourism comprises of 4.25% of the gross domestic product (GDP) and 7% of employment share.

CONCLUSION

The CORONA global pandemic has created havoc and an unprecedented economic bearing on global economics, demand and supply disruption, etc. The virulence and the severity of the spread of the virus is so acute that it has caused a lot of job loss, unemployment, temporary shutdown of manufacturing output, and reduction in the consumption expenditure by people.

The CORONA outbreak has also brought a hard effect on the travel and tourism industry due to the temporary travel ban imposed by most of the countries. Tourism food services, transportation, entertainment, and hotel business are the main industries that would face the heat of the crisis. The economic costs in terms of tourism revenue out of this pandemic outbreak will continue to mount if the further spread of the virus is not taken care of. Methods like complete lockdown of the city and hard quarantine measures adopted by various countries are mostly a difficult affair for a third-world country like India, especially in Kerala.

Bibliography

- Anbumathy, M. Mary. "The Impact of Covid-19 On Tourism Industry with Special Reference to Kerala." *EFFLATOUNIA-Multidisciplinary Journal* 5.2 (2021).
- Chandran, Priya, and V. Johnson. "AYURVEDIC HEALTH TOURISM IN KERALA."
- Dr Nikita Arora and Vaishnavi Gupta, Study on Impact of COVID-19 on Indian Economy, International Journal of Science and Research (IJSR) ISSN: 2319-7064 Research Gate Impact Factor, 2018.
- Goult, Elizabeth, et al. "COVID-19 in Kerala: analysis of measures and impacts." (2020).
- Jeemon Jacob, Covid-19: Kerala tourism sector hit hard by the pandemic, India Today, June 9, 2021.
- Kerala Tourist Statistics 2019
- KM, Siby, V. Varghese, and Shiju CR. "The Economic Impact Of Covid-19 Pandemic On The Travel And Tourism Industry: Kerala Evidence." (2021): 1491-1497.
- Report Malayala Manorama.
- Roy, Annet Sara, et al. "A STUDY ON IMPACT OF COVID-19 ON TOURISM SECTOR-A SPECIAL STUDY ON KUMARAKOM." (2021).
- Sreejith, S. "Report on Socio-Economic Impact of COVID 19 on Migrant Workers with Reference to Kerala State." *Journal of Contemporary Issues in Business and Government* 27.1 (2021): 686-707.

CHAPTER 8

TOURISM SECTOR: COVID-19'S IMPACT AND SURVIVAL IN THE FACE OF COVID-19 WITH SPECIAL REFERENCE TO KERALA

Vidhya Vijayan P,
Research Scholar, PG
Department of Commerce and Research Centre,
Mahatma Gandhi College, Trivandrum,

Dr Reshmi R Prasad,
Principal, All Saints' College,
Trivandrum,

ABSTRACT:

COVID-19 had a massive impact everywhere across the world. Majority of the world's countries went behind lockdown, and human life was confined to the four walls of the home. All most all the industries were strongly affected and the tourism sector was not exempted. Many constraints have been placed on the tourism and hospitality sectors, and many countries closed their borders. Kerala, amongst the most prominent tourist destinations and known as "God's own Country," was also strongly affected by COVID, resulting in a huge drop in revenue. Without government support, rehabilitation of the sector is more or less impossible. In this chapter, the impact of COVID-19 on Kerala's tourism sector as well as the government's efforts to relaunch the travel and tourism business is explored.

Keywords: Covid 19 pandemic, Lockdown, Tourism industry, and Government initiatives

INTRODUCTION:

From the beginning of coronavirus breakout in the Wuhan district of China in late 2019, alarms about the virus's global spread were raised. The pandemic's impact was severely underestimated in the initial days of the virus transmission, gradually it devastated many nations around the world. Since 1950, the travel economy has expanded at a steady and rapid rate. As per the World Travel and Tourism Council's Annual Competitiveness Report on Tourism (2019), the tourism industry equates to roughly 10% of global GDP. On a global scale, this industry has created only one out of four occupations within last five years. International travel was expanding, according to the United Nations World Tourism Organization's Reed Travel Exhibitions Report (2020), with only about 1.5 billion passengers travelling globally. The tourism sector contributes $1.7 trillion to the economy (7 percent of the total value of world goods and services). The pandemic attack has resulted in a dramatic drop in international tourist arrivals, decreasing worldwide tourism receipts to somewhere around one-third of the $1.7 trillion generated in 2019. The virus has had an adverse influence on tour operations and travel agency firms everywhere around the world. Advance ticket bookings, hotel reservations, and tour packages had to be cancelled, and the money refunded to the customers. India, the United Kingdom, Germany, and Spain have all been put on complete lockdown over almost three months, which had a significant impact on business. Kerala is one of India's best-known leisure and tourism destinations, and it has been significantly damaged by COVID-19 plague.

TOURISM INDUSTRY IN KERALA:

Kerala is one of India's most popular tourist destinations, positioned on the tropical Malabar coast in south-western India. Kerala is one of the few states that really has successfully marketed its natural beauty to the leisure tourism market. Tourists from all around the world have indeed been drawn to the state by its unique heritage and cultural diversity. As per BBC travel assessments, Kerala has to be the most major tourist attraction among overseas tourists in 2018. Kerala is notable for its ecotourism development and gorgeous backwaters, and has also been named one of the ten paradises of the world by National Geographic Traveler. Kerala is one of the most popular tourist destinations in the world owing to its special culture and traditions, and even its diverse culture. The tourism industry, which is expanding at a rate of 13.31 percent, is a major contributor to the state's economy. Kerala was a widely undefined destination until the early 1980s, with most of the strong tourism circuits concentrated in the north. The Kerala Tourism Development Corporation (the government organization in charge of the state's tourism prospects) undertook aggressive marketing campaigns that lay the foundation for the tourism industry's boom. Kerala Tourism continued to build itself into one of India's specialized holiday destinations in the decades that followed. Kerala — God's Own Country became a global super brand and has been used in tourism campaigns. Kerala is renowned among the most well-known tourist hotspots. Kerala attracted 660,000 tourists from around the world in 2010.

Tourism has grown to a leading sector of the Kerala economy, with a growing emphasis in terms of job creation and economic growth (GOK, 2002). The directorate general perceives tourism as one of the few prospects for stimulating the economy, especially considering the manufacturing sector's limited opportunities, troubles in the agricultural and traditional sectors, and the mystery surrounding expatriate working in the Persian Gulf (Pushpangadan, 2003). Kerala would be seen as a model for other Indian states to adopt in its footsteps. Kerala's tourism sector rose exponentially in the 1990s and beyond, and it is predicted to continue to be there in the future. Kerala's proportion of international tourists entering India has grown from 5.54 percent in 1994 to 8.85 percent in 2005, making it the nation's largest tourism state. Tourism earnings are also anticipated to widen at a tremendous speed of more than 23.5 percent, which is substantially higher than India's and the worldwide average earnings economic performance of 14.3 percent and 6.5 percent, respectively. Tourism receipts from international tourists had risen dramatically during this time span, ranging from 1.16 billion rupees in 1994 to 19.89 billion rupees in 2006. (GOK, 2006a). Kerala's international tourist arrivals reached almost 500,000 in 2006, and are anticipated to cross 500,000 by 2007. Kerala is becoming one of the world's fastest growing destinations, with an average annual arrival growth rate of 18 percent for domestic tourists and 12 percent for international tourists (WTTC, 2002).

COVID 19 AND ITS IMPACT ON TOURISM INDUSTRY:

The COVID-19 pandemic, also known as the coronavirus pandemic, has created havoc on every aspect of life and has had a catastrophic impact on the economy. The tourism sector in Kerala was severely devastated by the pandemic. The COVID-19 pandemic struck at the pinnacle of the travel and tourism industry. Kerala's tourist economy is in jeopardy, having lost three seasons in a row for the first time due to the pandemic. Tour operators remain uncertain when the pandemic will expire and the industry will rebound to its glorious past, when it delivered 10% of the state's GDP and offered 23.5 percent of total employment. The outbreak spread rapidly and grabbed the country that it put the nation on lockdown, throwing a shock to every portion of the economy. The epidemic has cost the tourism industry Rs. 35000 Crore in revenues. In a debt trap, tour operators see no way out. With the district entangled in the pandemic dragnet, Alappuzha, Kerala's houseboat heartland, appeared to be a haunted destination. On the Vembanad lake, approximately 1,200 houseboats are docked. They've been moored since over 16 months, and the majority of them are in poor condition. As per the Kerala Tourism Department, tourist arrivals in 2020 dipped by around 73 percent compared to the previous year to just over 53 lakh visitors, with 94 percent of which were domestic tourists. As a result, tourism revenue dropped from almost Rs. 45,000 Crore (12 percent of GDP) in 2019 to just under Rs. 10,000 Crore in 2020. The tenacious run of COVID-19's second wave has cast a long shadow over Kerala's tourism aspirations, one of the country's most beautiful places to visit.

SURVIVAL AFTER COVID 19:

The impact of the COVID-19 pandemic is still being felt in Kerala, but the healing process has begun. The Kerala government's numerous departments are putting on a united front to battle the pandemic. Kerala's hospitality department nowadays is analyzing the situation in order to devise an effective strategy for aiding the sector in tackling the problems. Kerala Tourism seeks to implement short-haul tours beyond COVID-19, with such a focus on domestic tourism. The intention is to promote the state's most famous tourist attractions aggressively. Kerala Tourism is also looking to offer "learning experiences" as component of its packages. The Responsible Tourism (RT) Mission would be used to design this experimental method. It does provide holidaymakers with the opportunity to observe a Kerala trade, art, or martial art while staying in the state. The bio-bubble system and the completely vaccinated destination initiative have helped the state's tourism sector, which had been crippled by that of the pandemic outbreak, recoup its tourist inflow. During the crisis, the state government's entire priority was on rebuilding trust in the sector, with the mission of "Safe Kerala, Safe Tourism." As part of this, several programmes were launched to real drawback vacationers. In the Wayanad district's Vythiri, the fully vaccinated destination project was launched. This has since been replicated to other regions, with the majority of tourism destinations currently having met the goal. The "bio-bubble" system has been implemented to ensure the protection of the tourism business. Innovative initiatives such as caravan tourism and the farm tourism network, a proposed programme to leverage agriculture's potential which was recently developed by the Kerala Tourism Department, are aiding in the recovery of the Kerala tourism industry.

VARIOUS REVIVAL PLANS FOR TRAVEL AND TOURISM SECTOR BY INDIAN GOVERNMENT:

➤ All divisions of the tourism industry are hunting for a means of making ends meet and are waiting for interim relief to pay salaries, EMIs, interest, as well as other expenses. The banks have already confirmed that all banks and non-banking commercial institutions (NBFCs) are eligible for such a three-month borrowing moratorium. The Indian Confederation of Commerce (ICC) recommended that, reflecting the enormity of the destruction, the government should extend this for at least further six months

➤ In addition, the ICC proposed that all principle and interest payments, along with tax payments, be halted for six to nine months. Advances and overdrafts should be prolonged as well.

➤ The ICC also recommended that the tourism industry be given a complete Goods and Service Tax (GST) holiday for a period of 12 months in order to guarantee its preservation.

➤ The Indian government, for its own part, announced a special compensation package 1.7 lakh crore (Indian Rupees) for COVID-19-affected sectors

➤ Following the coronavirus epidemic, the ICC urged that the Reserve Bank of India (RBI) ease the working capital bottleneck in India's tourism sector. In addition, the ICC suggested that banks approve financing speedier for the Indian tourist industry, particularly for the benefit of the travel and hotel segments.

CONCLUSION:

Covid 19 has wreaked havoc on every walk of society, dragging not only the Indian economy to a crawl but the rest of the world to a standstill. Tourism and tourism-related industries, along with their employees, are some of the worst-affected industries. The tourism sector's revenue decreased to a significant level as a result of the Covid 19 outbreak, and government aid is now becoming extremely important. Kerala's government recently declared a range of initiatives aiming at revitalizing the tourist economy. Despite the fact that Covid 19 has generated multiple problems, it has also presented a potential for reassessment in some areas. The current economic downturn provides a chance to redefine tourism in the future. Tourism is at a fork in the road, and the policies implemented today will determine tourism in the future. While capitalizing on digitization, supporting the low-carbon transition, and fostering the structural transformation required to establish a stronger, more sustainable, and resilient tourism economy, the government must recognize the long-term repercussions of the crisis.

REFERENCES:

➤ Sandhya H (2021). The Survival of Travel and Tourism Industry amidst the Covid 19 Pandemic – Challenges and Opportunities of the Indian Tourism Sector. Atna Journal of Tourism Studies. 16(1). 41-66.

➤ Ding, W., Levine, R., Lin, C., Xie, W., (2020). Corporate Immunity to the COVID-19 Pandemic (No. w27055). National Bureau of Economic Research.

➤ Kaushal, & Srivastava. (2020). Hospitality and tourism industry amid COVID-19 pandemic: Perspectives on challenges and learnings from India. International Journal of Hospitality Management. https://doi.org/ 10.1016/j.ijhm.2020.102707

➤ Kumar (2020). Disastrous impact of Coronavirus (COVID 19) on Tourism and Hospitality Industry in India. Journal of Xi'an University of Architecture & Technology, 12(5), 698 -712.

➤ Larissa Neuburger & Roman Egger (2020): Travel risk perception and travel behaviour during the COVID-19 pandemic 2020: a case study of the DACH region, Current Issues in Tourism, DOI: 10.1080/13683500.2020.1803807

CHAPTER 9

IMPACT OF COVID-19 ON TOURISM SECTOR IN KERALA

Dr. Reji Vargheese Mekkaden,
Associate Professor, Department of Political Science,
St. George's College Aruvithura, Kottayam

ABSTRACT

COVID-19 epidemic broke out when the journey and tourism industry was at its mount. There was a trend among the new generation outlaying further time and money on recreational conditioning as stress relievers. Trip and Tourism were prominent conditioning in this regard. The spread of the epidemic was so quick and gripping that the country itself got into complete lockdown and consequent shocks in every aspect of the economy. The study tried to dissect the changes that passed in the trip and tourism industriousness as a result of the epidemic. The study inferred from the analysis that lockdowns due to the Covid 19 epidemic had significant and enduring negative impacts on the business prospects of stakeholders in the passage and tourism industry.

Key Words: - Tourism and Covid -19, Trip, impact of Covid 19

INTRODUCTION

Tourism is the exercise of people traveling to and staying in places outside their usual surroundings for rest, business or other purposes for not further than one successive time. Tourism may be a dynamic and competitive industry that needs the power to condition constantly to guests' changing requirements and desires, as the client's satisfaction, safety and enjoyment are particularly the focus of tourism businesses. Trip is as old as humanity on the world. The man at the morning of his actuality floated about the face of the earth in the hunt of food, shelter, securities and better niche. Now, it is one of the world's swift- growing diligence with a serious exchange and employment generation for several countries. It' is one of the most foremost remarkable, profitable and social flashes.

Kerala (God's own Country) has mind-blowing sightseer destinations. People from colorful corridor of the country and also from colorful corridor of the world visit Kerala for its beautiful decors and awful places. Kerala is fabulous for its unique culture and traditions, combined with its varied demography. This has made Kerala, one of the most popular sightseer destinations in the world tourism.

TOURISM AND COVID-19

The COVID-19 epidemic has caused significant dislocations in the global economy. By the COVID-19 epidemic had brought multinational passage to an abrupt halt and significantly impacted the tourism industry. COVID-19 leads to health issues and profitable extremity on worldwide scale. While little is understood at this point about numerous aspects of the complaint, it's generally agreed that the virus is freely transmittable and that the death rate is low in comparison to former epidemics similar as SARS, Ebola and the bubonic plague. Victims are heavily disposed towards aged people and those with being affections. To decelerate the spread of the germicide, multiple countries have encouraged or commanded the use of germfree practices similar as hand washing, social (spatial) distancing and isolation. Government have introduced a slew of policy measures similar as targeted testing and tracking, lockdown measures, upgrading public health installations and check of borders. The measures have impacted numerous industries and the delivery of private services, leading demand and give side shocks.

SECOND WAVE OF COVID-19 WORSENS TOURISM WOES OF KERALA

The tourism industry contributes 12 percent to the state's GDP. Though the govt. tied up with numerous banks for loan schemes to revive the sector, the response has been poor. In fact, indeed after the government said it will pay 50% interest charges, banks are reluctant to advance, fearing defaults. The unrelenting run of the alternate surge of COVID-19 has cast a shadow over the tourism prospects of Kerala, one of the premier trip destinations in the country. Formerly, the epidemic has reduced traveler business to a trickle last time. Now, the alternate surge has ruined the state's chance of soliciting callers with its monsoon charm. With the future looking uncertain as the Test Positivity Rate (TPR) continues to rule high, industry stakeholders are keeping their fritters crossed as the main tourist season approaches.

The main tourism season in Kerala starts from October and stretches to February, when both multinational and domestic travelers arrive. In April and May, there's a rush of domestic travelers because of summer holiday. Monsoon tourism, promoted between June and August, has drawn little response after the 2018 floods. Coming as it did after one of worst deluges in the state's history, COVID-19 dealt a heavy blow to traveler flux.

HOSTEL INDUSTRY STRUGGLING TO MEET EXPENSES

The hostel industry is stumbling to meet the charges, with the tourist inflow dipping sharply. We've to keep a shell staff for conservation. Either, there are current charges and payment of loans and taxes. We're paying a subsistence amount to the staff remaining at home. This could be a huge burden for small players, which has properties in several traveler destinations in the state. The hotels witnessed a rush of original callers when restrictions were eased after September last time. But it was hardly sufficient to run the property. The advents stopped when the lockdown was assessed following the alternate wave of the epidemic in May. The lockdown in the weekends and category of places grounded on the intensity of the spread of the complaint have nearly stopped people from traveling.

A HOUSE BOAT ON THE BACKWATERS OF KERALA

Alappuzha, the home of the houseboat industry in Kerala, looks like a haunted destination now, with the district caught in the epidemic dragnet. Around houseboats lie anchored on the Vembanad Lake. They've been fixed there for the once 16 months and a maturity of them is in no practical condition. The houseboat industry is just one part of it; the tourism sector itself is in peril in Kerala having lost three successive seasons for the first time due to the epidemic. Tour drivers have no idea when the epidemic will end and the sector will get back to its old tone when it contributed 10% of the state's GDP and offered 23.5% of the total employment.

It had realizes that for at least another two times foreign traveler incomings will be at a minimum. During the once 24 times, God's own Country had shown significant growth in the tourism sector even as industry and others lagged. The two successive floods in 2018 and 2019, and now the Covid-19 epidemic, smoothed the tourism sector. After the 2018 mega cataracts, the state reported the loftiest growth rate in domestic and foreign sightseer advents in the last 24 times. There was around 8.5 per cent growth in foreign and 17.8 per cent growth in domestic sightseer advents in 2019 compared to 2018. The global promotional campaigns, new enterprise like introducing new destinations to multinational bloggers and developing event destinations helped the state to achieve this unique growth. With the epidemic, we've lost all our earnings.

Around millions of domestic and millions of foreign travelers visited Kerala in 2019. Since the state reported its first Covid positive case on January 2020, only foreign excursionists visited in the time, a 61 per cent decline in numbers compared to the former time. Domestic traveler incomings also drastically declined by performing in total losses of cores in 2020. There's maximum confusion in the tourism assiduity as we've no idea when we can renew business operations. The houseboat industry has incurred colossal losses; a maturity of the boats will bear heavy investments in repairs before they can be launched again. All of boat proprietor had invested their gains in the history and taken loans to roll out business. So has lost everything as the boats are completely damaged after remaining fixed in the water for the last 16 months. The state government has requested to advertise a moratorium on the loans and is staying for a response. The debt trap could lead to family tragedies as we've no money to spend of people in the houseboat industry.

The houseboat holders said that Covid 19 has destabilized the sector fully and it may have to stay tillmid-2024 to renew operations completely. It may take another two times for foreign travelers to flock to Kerala again. Till losses will accumulate, it took nearly 25 times of goodwill to turn Kerala into God's own Country for the travelers.

The boat motorist after unlock, industry picked up the pace but now again travelers aren't coming as cases are adding. We are returning to the situation that was during the lockdown the tourism industry, which was on the revival path of post lockdown, is yet again staring at another crisis due to the spurt in Covid-19 cases. Several travelers are avoiding traveling to' traveler locations in the state worrying that a lockdown is likely to be charged in the near future.

HOUSEBOATS HAVE ONLY ORIGINAL VISITORS

Houseboat holders are grappling with another problem cost of fuel. "From around Rs 60 per liter before COVID, diesel cost has zoomed to nearly Rs 100 adding to the cost. In the absence of travelers from other countries or from outside the country, these boats are now mostly plying original callers at discounted rates for a many hours. Unless there's a moratorium on loans and grant of interest, it would be sticky for the several hundreds of houseboats, primarily in Alappuzha quarter, to survive, especially with little stopgap of transnational travelers arriving this time too, Mathew said. Foreign travelers bring further profit. But the last foreign visitant we had was in March 2019.

SUGGESTIONS

The COVID-19 extremity has fully altered the travel and tourism economy, oppressively impacting people's livelihoods and businesses. As the epidemic continues to evolve, the full consequences for the tourism frugality aren't yet clear. Still, a return to business as usual' is doubtful. Policy makers will need to learn from the COVID-19 extremity to make a stronger, more flexible tourism frugality for the future.

Trip insurance in this expression refers to guarding trippers from trip cancellation to flight detainments and icing backing for medical exigency or baggage loss. Still, when the cases containing CREDIT CARD, FULL REFUND, and Trip AGENCY were examined, it was observed that the commentary were about the refund of all or some part of the payments, and change or cancellation of trip plans. More packages the government should insure better packages for the world travelers by serving a safe trip terrain and reducing legal restrictions at least to some extent. Governments need threat- grounded results grounded on sound scientific evidence to safely lift travel restrictions and get the multinational tourism ecosystem back over and running. These results also need to be doable to apply, with sufficient capacity available to insure these systems are can serve reliably. Continued government support will be demanded to insure destinations and tourism businesses continued government support will be demanded to give tourism services to meet demand when the recovery comes, and formerly starting to address the long term implications of the extremity. It'll be important to work with tourism businesses so they're sustainable beyond the end of the supports. This support needs to be decreasingly conditioned on broader environmental, profitable and social objects. Measures to support innovation and stimulate investment will be needed, to maintain capacity, restore the attractiveness of the destination, bolster the quality and competitiveness of the tourism offer, and improve the prospects for sustainable recovery.

Sustainability should be a core guiding principle in the recovery. Before the crisis, the need for policy makers to work with industry and communities to strike a balance between the economic, environmental and social benefits and costs associated with tourism development, and implement a long-term and sustainable vision for the future. This imperative remains, with health and safety considerations more prominent, together with the added need to limit tourism as a vector of the pandemic. Countries were already moving in this direction before the crisis, developing national tourism strategies and policies based on sustainable tourism development principles.

CONCLUSION

The tourism sector has been the worst hit and the state government has announced a package to revive the industry, focusing more on domestic travelers. We hope the situation will improve after the state is fully vaccinated. Meanwhile, the government has convened a meeting of all industry stakeholders to understand the gravity of the situation and take remedial measures.

Tourism helps in preserving the culture by visiting the local places which still live by the old rules. It is utmost duty of the tourism industry to promote responsible tourism and take actions accordingly in order to better develop the industry. From the study, it is concluded that, COVID 19 has considerable impact in both environment and economic factors. It is found that COVID 19 has positive environment impact such as reduced pollution, water in falls and dams became purified, cleanliness is witnessed, overall environmental development and nature becomes more beautiful. And COVID 19 has negative economic impact such as collapse of the tourism industry, decrease in income, rise in unemployment, reduced income to the government and stress on supply chains. This study reveals that, COVID 19 has positive impact on nature and negative impact on economy.

REFERENCES

- Gopinath, Gita (2020), "The Great Lockdown: Worst Economic Downturn Since the Great Depression", IMFBlog, 14 April 2020,

- International Monetary Fund (IMF), available at: https://blogs.imf.org/2020/04/14/the-great-lockdown-worsteconomic-downturn-since-the-great-depression/ Government of Kerala (2020) Budget in Brief 2020-21, Government of Kerala, Thiruvananthapuram.

- Kerala State Planning Board (KSPB) (2014), Perspective Plan 2030 – Kerala Vol I to IV, Government of Kerala, Thiruvananthapuram.

- Kerala State Planning Board (KSPB) (2020), Economic Review 2019, Volume I & II, Government of Kerala, Thiruvananthapuram.

- National Statistical Office (NSO) (2019), Annual Report – Periodic Labour Force Survey (PLFS), July 2017--June 2018, New Delhi.

- Prakash, B. A (2020), Local Finance, Fiscal Decentralisation and Decentralised Planning: A Kerala Experience, Sage Publications, New Delhi.

- World Bank (2020), "Global Economic Prospects: Analytical Chapters", A World bank Group Flagship Report, June 2020, International Bank for Reconstruction and Development/The World Bank, Washington.

CHAPTER 10

PERCEPTION AND SATISFACTION OF TOURISTS TOWARDS A GREEN TOURISM DESTINATION: WITH SPECIAL REFERENCE TO MANGO MEADOWS AGRICULTURAL THEME PARK IN KERALA

Dr. Raji Mohan
Assistant Professor
PG Department of Commerce and Research Centre
St. Xavier's College for Women, Aluva

Remya Hari
Research Scholar
PG Department of Commerce and Research Centre
St. Xavier's College for Women, Aluva

ABSTRACT:

Different stakeholders of tourism are giving more attention to green tourism due to its environmental benefits. Research studies concentrating behavioural aspect of tourist towards sustainability of green tourism is not fully exhausted. The present study tries to explore perception and satisfaction of tourist towards green tourism practices followed in the first agricultural theme park in Kerala. The scope of the study is limited to Mango Meadows Agricultural Theme Park, Kaduthuruthi, Kottayam. Since the study was conducted during post covid period, only domestic tourists constitute the population. Data for the study was collected through primary sources with the help of a structured questionnaire. Collected data analysed by descriptive statistics including percentage, mean and median. The results shows that majority of the tourists are satisfied by the services in the destination. It also suggests adoption of green tourism practices in other destinations of Kerala.

Keywords: Green tourism, Climate change, sustainability, destination

INTRODUCTION

Today climate change is the most pressing issue facing humanity. Floods, hurricanes, earthquake, fires have overtaken news headlines recently. We have to ensure that future growth is in balance with our planet. As tourism, a transversal sector interacting with many other industries and services, even a small improvement towards sustainability will have important impacts in the shift towards more sustainable, cleaner and low carbon economic growth. Transportation, a major source of greenhouse gases, is an indispensable part of tourism. We cannot stop travel in the mindset of saving our planet. However, to lesson our travel footprint in a meaningful way we can change our behaviour of travelling in a meaningful way by involving energy efficient vehicles in our trips, supporting accommodations investing in green practices, look for local food, buy local products, buy non-plastic reusable products, etc. The development of green tourism is a proven world practice adopted to fight against the issue in the sector.

A destination can flourish only by delivering quality services and improving customer satisfaction. "According to Wang et. al. (2009), tourist's satisfaction is a feeling that generate through the cognitive and emotional aspects of tourism activities. It is mainly based on the tourist's expectations, destination image, perceived quality and perceived value". "If the tourists can meet their exact needs during the holiday consumption in the destination, they will be satisfied, otherwise will be dissatisfied. Whereas when the holiday experiences exceed the tourist's expectation, they will be delighted (Gnanapala, 2012)". The paper tries to examine the relationship between customers perception and quality of service they actually received at tourist destination.

Tourists an indispensable element of tourism and it is necessary that they have to be involved in the process as well. For proper implementation of green measures in a tourist spot, it is necessary to know about the awareness, responsibility and acceptance of such measures by them. It is necessary to assess the perception of tourists with regard to attributes of a destination is whether sustainable or not. It is also necessary to study about understandability of tourists towards green tourism and also their ability to identify values related to it in a destination. Kerala, culturally rich and diverse land accounts for a considerable amount of tourists influx every year. Mango Meadows, brought pride to Kerala for being the best example of conserving the environment. Even though, Kerala was rattled by Covid pandemic in its second wave, Government boosts the confidence level of the sector by fostering domestic tourism in post covid period. In the case of a domestic tourists, a property that truly channels and reflects its locations essence in its décor, settings and food stands out more than a generic modern aesthetic. This paper tries to explore the perception and satisfaction of domestic tourists towards the green practices followed in Mango Meadows, an agricultural theme park in Kerala.

OBJECTIVES OF THE STUDY

> To examine green tourism practices followed in Mango meadows

> To analyse tourist's perception and its role in identifying values related green tourism in a destination

> To measure the overall satisfaction received by tourists in the destination.

METHODOLOGY

The study design adopts an exploratory research approach for assessing tourist perception and satisfaction towards mango meadows. The sample size is restricted to 48 samples due to obvious constraints of covid pandemic. Primary data collected through a structured questionnaire and convenient sampling method was used. For analysing the data Statistical Package for Social Science (SPSS) is used by using descriptive statistics with percentage analysis, mean and standard deviation.

LITERATURE REVIEW

Susanne Becken (2004) said that tourist icons are major pull factors which attract attention of potential tourists. However, overemphasis on tourist icons ultimately leads to unsustainable tourism development like tourist travel long distance to visit spatially very dispersed tourist icons results in considerable amount of greenhouse gas emissions. The paper also reveals the importance of experience focused promotion which envisages that tourists will stay longer and thereby also spend more. It helps to decrease pressure on tourist icons and enable regions to participate in tourism development. Weijing Zhao examined tourist's perception of the sustainable tourism development and pointed out that tourism destinations should tailor their offering specifically meet needs of each category of tourist with sustainability as the main objective. He also points collaboration of local government private sector and other local stakeholders in planning and formulation of rules and guidelines restrict tourist's behaviour and also to protect the predominant quality of the area. He recommends the adoption of green tourism programmes to raise tourist awareness about the importance of environment and need to conserve natural resources and beauty of the area. Begum Aydin et.al (2020) points out that understanding consumers views concerning the sustainability of tourist's destination pivotal in order to support responsible tourism practices. He also suggested creation of tourist-based sustainability model so that destinations can focus on elements of sustainability that directly affect tourists experience such as conservation of the environment and local culture. Juan Ignacio Pulido et. al viewed that for a destination to be able to advance in terms of sustainability, it is not just to implement supply policies, it is also necessary that the tourists are to be involved in the process as well. He also points out that demand policies must be developed to ensure a greater awareness and responsibility of tourists in the destinations they visit.

MANGO MEADOWS- WORLDS FIRST AGRICULTURAL THEME PARK

Mango Meadows is a man-made green paradise spread over 30 acres of land. It is the result of over 15 years of hard work of N K Kurien, a gulf returnee. He invested all his earnings in this novel initiative. He reminds everyone that environment conservation is the responsibility of each and every person by teaching the world that nothing can become a barrier if there is dedication to conserve the environment. He proved it by creating this wonder in Upper Kuttanad, a land lies below sea level. Mango Meadows at Ayamkudi is a small hamlet near Kaduthuruthy in Kerala's Kottayam, claims to be the world's first agricultural theme park. It is built on what was once just a piece of barren land with a few coconut trees. But it now accommodates 4800 species of plants from 15 countries. This includes 700 trees, 900 flowering plants around 64 varieties of fish, and almost all domestic animals and birds. The Park is known to have more than 1950 species of medicinal plants. There are four ponds in the park that are replete with fish. These ponds are interconnected so that the fish can move freely. This Theme Park has found a place in the Limca book of Records for replica of rich bio diversity. A walk via sinuous walkways leading through a wide variety of flora and fauna gives a peaceful experience for the visitors. An awe-inspiring organic vegetable farm is also main attraction of the destination which accounts for production of different kinds of fruits and vegetables. The heart-warming refreshment stalls in mango meadows give an opportunity for kids to know about village life. A section called village craft enable the tourists to experience artistic pottery skills. Kids can get familiarised with animal planets by encouraging them to feed animals and to make them realize their contribution to mankind. Addressing less carbon footprints in the destination it also gives facilities of electric buggies for travelling inside the park. The Park also offers conventional delicacies to customers prepared with organic, garden-fresh vegetables.

GREEN TOURISM

Green tourism is a moniker for a wide range of related concepts including ecotourism, nature tourism, adventure tourism, environmental tourism, new tourism sustainable tourism and others (Goelder and Ritchie, 2003). Green tourism means the practices followed in the tourist's destinations to protect the environment and maintain those places for a long period. It takes into account the needs of the environment, local residents, businesses and visitors. It covers any tourism whether large or small and rural or urban. The main focus of green tourism is reducing the negative impacts of tourism rather than using the term as a marketing tool. The main practices followed in green tourism destinations are;

- ➤ Promotion of green or environmentally friendly products
- ➤ Creation of zero wastage zones for concentrating tourists spots garbage free
- ➤ Wide acceptability to local products
- ➤ Reuse of material and recycling programmes
- ➤ Education and training programmes
- ➤ Water efficiency and maintenance practices
- ➤ Displaying green protocols used

FINDINGS AND DISCUSSION

In accordance with the purpose of the study, the data were collected from

48 respondents through direct personal interview. Due to covid protocol only limited number of respondents are allowed to enter the park in a day. The main findings of the study are as follows:

Table 1: Demographic profile and visiting details of the respondents

	Frequency	Percentage
1. Gender		
Male	19	39.6
Female	29	60.4
2. Age		
15-24	25	52.1
25-34	7	1.6
35-44	7	14.6
45-54	4	8.3
55-64	3	6.2
Above 65	2	4.2
3. Number of Visit		
First time	33	68.8
2-3 times	13	27.1
More than 3	2	4.2
4. Source of Information		
Friends & Relatives	29	60.4
News paper	3	6.2
Social Media	10	20.8
Tourism Information Centre	1	2.1
Others	5	10.4

Table 1 reveals that among the respondents 60% are female and 40% are males. Majority of the visitors fall between the age group of 15-24. Among them 68% of visitors are visiting the destination for the first time and 27% of visitors have visited 2-3 times. Around 60% of the visitors know about the destination through friends and relatives, 20% through social media and 10% through other sources.

Table 2: Factors influenced tourists in visiting the destination

Factors influenced	Frequency	Percentage
Experiencing greenic beauty, Biodiversity and Organic farming	17	35.4
Environment friendly services	12	25.0
Back to root experience for kids	7	14.5
Preservation of Culture and guidance	8	16.6
Traditional and local food	4	8.3

This table shows the factors which attracted tourists towards the destination. Among them greenic beauty places first. It gives tourists a place for actively participating in agriculture and farming related activities, which the young generation heard only in stories. Tourists are not much attracted about local and traditional food. It may be as a result of most of the destinations are now giving focus on delivering local and traditional food to their visitors. Since new generation kids are growing more and more tech savvy, some parents are attracted for delivering their kids a back root experience, which they have experienced in their childhood days.

Table 3: Tourists Satisfaction with green tourism elements and Overall satisfaction

Variables	Mean	Std deviation
Preservation of Landscape and Greenic beauty	4.21	0.968
Guidance & courtesy of staff	3.87	0.897
Food &Amenities	3.19	0.987
Culture & Art promotion	3.27	0.789
Cleanliness &Waste Disposal mechanism	4.01	0.952
Overall satisfaction	3.91	0.964

Tourists were generally satisfied with Mango Meadows as a destination with a mean of 3.91 and the likelihood of tourists recommending the destination with a high Mean of 4.21. As most of the tourists come to the destination on the recommendation of friends and relatives, the findings argues well that higher satisfaction of tourists is influential in spreading a word of mouth. Even there was a less mean rank in food and amenities, all other variables make the destination highly satisfiable. As shown in the table lowest value of the standard deviation is 0.789 and the highest value is 0.987. This means that values are not equally distributed and therefore the respondents were differing in their response. As most of them belong to young category their satisfaction level also be differ as each person is different from other. Tourists are welcomed to the destination with an introductory section, which gives an information about the features and practices followed in the destination.

CONCLUSION

Mango Meadows, venture of a single man is well relatively given contribution towards delivering sustainable tourism practices in a destination. The results shows that greenic beauty and bio diversity, calm and peaceful ambience, participation in farm fresh and agriculture related activities, experiencing culture and art related activities, green motoric skill programmes, hospitality and guidance given by the staff etc gives a new experience for tourists. It also adds that most of the visitors were young ones below 45 age groups, which shows that the young generation gives due importance in visiting sustainable tourism destinations. Tourists felt that a day is not enough to experience the facilities, they prefer to extend the visiting time. Since some of the rides are special paid ones, especially electric vehicles, in addition to entry ticket makes tourists less comfortable. However, it is not much expensive when compare to the benefits received from it in terms of nature. Like virtually everything the ranging pandemic casted a shadow over the very existence of the destination. Government assistance is to be provided to safeguard the destination from reducing its struggles. A crowd funding initiative was taken now to save the park with the help of a committee including Kaduthuruthy legislator Mons Joseph and Mahatma Gandhi University Vice Chancellor, Sabu Thomas. Local and State Government should take necessary steps to protect the destination from being closed down. Government can also adopt the policies adopted by this destination in other destinations which gives due contribution towards minimising carbon footprints.

REFERENCES

➤   Athula Gnanapala, (2015), Tourist's perception and satisfaction: Implications for

Destination Management, American Journal of Marketing Research, Vol. 1, No.1, pp7-19.

> Begum Aydin et. al. (2020), Understanding the tourist's perspectives of Sustainability in Cultural Tourist Destinations, Sustainability 2, MDPI.

> Goeldner, C. R.,et. al., (2003). *Tourism: principles, practices, philosophies.* John Wiley & Son (New Jersey).

> John R M Philemon, (2015) Assessment of tourist's perception and satisfaction of Tanzania Destination, European Scientific Journal, vol. 11, no.13, ISSN :1857-7881, pp 107-119

> Juan Ignacio Pulido- Fernandez et. al., (2014), Perception of sustainability of a tourism destination: analysis from tourist's expectation, International Business & Economics Research Journal, Vol. 13, No.7, pp1587—1598.

> Kadek Dwi Cahaya Putra, et al, (2019) An Importance-Performance Analysis of Bali State Polytechnic's Green Tourism Program, Advances in Social Science, Education and Humanities Research volume 54, pp 286-291.

> Ravinder Jangra, et al. (2021) An analysis of tourist's perception towards tourism development: study of cold desert destination, India, Geography and Sustainability2, pp 48-58.

> Satish Chandra Bagri, et. al, (2015), Tourist's satisfaction at Trijuginarayan, India: An Importance- Performance analysis, Advances in Hospitality and Tourism Research, ISSN:2147-9100, Vol. 3(2), pp 89-115.

> Susanne Becken (2005), The role of tourist icons for sustainable tourism, Journal of Vacation Marketing, Vol. 11, No. 1, pp17-26.

> Sushila Devi Rajaratnam, et. al, (2014) Service Quality and previous experience as a moderator in determining tourist's satisfaction with rural tourism destinations in Malaysia: A partial least squares approach, 5th Asia Euro Conference 2014, Procedia Social and Behavioral Sciences144, pp 203-211, Science Direct, Elsevier

> Wang et al (2009), Consumer trust in tourism and Hospitality: A review of Literature, Journal of Hospitality and tourism management vol. 21, pp 1-9.

> Weijing Zhao (2014) Tourist's perception of sustainable tourism development of Tianzhu Mountain in Anhui Province, China, AU-GSB e- Journal Vol. 7, No. 1, pp 53-60.

CHAPTER 11

THE SHIFTING TRENDS IN TOURISM INDUSTRY:

THE INFLUENCE OF COVID-19 PANDEMIC, CONSUMER BEHAVIOUR AND TECHNOLOGICAL ADVANCEMENTS

Mishel Elizabeth Jacob
Research Scholar,
School of Management and Business Studies,
Mahatma Gandhi University
Kottayam

ABSTRACT:

The tourism industry has been recognized as one of the most vulnerable sectors that in the wake of any crisis. The global pandemic of Covid-19 has been no different. The disruption caused to the travel and tourism industry has been unprecedented. However, by adopting Covid protocols and also imbibing the latest technological advancement, this industry has is in the path of revival. This article briefly describes some of the shifting trends that the travel and tourism industry is witnessing.

Keywords: Trends, Covid-19, Artificial Intelligence, Staycation, IoT

INTRODUCTION

The novel and infectious Coronavirus (COVID-19) struck Wuhan in mid-December 2019, and within a short period it became a pandemic that engulfed the entire world (Yang et al., 2020). This disaster has been causing unprecedented changes in the structure and running of all industries around the world. The tourism industry has been recognized as one of the most vulnerable sectors that has been affected by this crisis (Mirzaei, et. al. 2019). According to the American Hotel & Lodging Association (2020), the hotel industry was the first to be negatively impacted by the pandemic, and will be the last one to recover, with nearly 3.9 million total hotel-supported jobs being lost. However, the world is learning to live with Covid-19 and therefore industries are adopting structural and transformative changes to work around COVID 19.

The major tourism trends post COVID-19 pandemic include focus on hygiene, safety, and local rather than international services, while also accelerating the use of contactless payments and remote working. It is important to follow the current tourism trends in response to increasing consumer actions as a result of the coronary pandemic. However, most patterns have arisen from more general shifts in customer behavior (Cohen, 2013). Therefore, this paper also enlists the changing trends in the tourism industry that has been brought about by general change in consumer attitude towards tourism (such as eco-travel) and the advancement in technology such as voice search, contactless payments and use of virtual reality and internet of things.

SAFETY & HYGIENE TOURISM TRENDS

Whether it is airlines, cruises, hotels, restaurants or bars, since the outbreak of COVID, safety and hygiene standards have been absolutely paramount (Mirzaei, et. al. 2019). With this in mind, there are a number of tourism trends that are related to this, such as increased cleaning, socially distanced seating, providing hand gel and enforcing masks in some settings.

This is also now a vital part of tourism marketing, with companies needing to make clear what their hygiene and safety policies are and what measures they are taking to keep customers safe. The threat of COVID has meant people are more reluctant to travel and visit tourism hot spots, so they will need to be persuaded that it is safe.

INCREASED EMPHASIS ON LEISURE

COVID has forced countries to adopt travel restrictions, while many businesses are encouraging employees to work from home and use video calling. As a result, business events have been particularly badly affected and one of the resulting tourism trends has been a switch in focus towards leisure customers (Abbas, et al., 2021). The pandemic has been hard on people and many are desperate for a holiday. Those businesses that were typically focused on business customers, are now focusing on families, couples, or groups of friends.

SHIFT FROM INTERNATIONAL TO LOCAL

The various travel restrictions and the reluctance of many people to travel abroad has meant many in the tourism industry are having to focus on local customers, rather than international ones (Sharma, et. al, 2021). This does not mean giving up on international travelers entirely, but it is likely to require a change in your core marketing strategies. With hotels, it could be best to highlight the kinds of facilities that may appeal to the local market, such as restaurant, gym facilities, Wi-Fi and even the fact that hotel rooms are ideal for remote work. Airlines and tourism management companies may also need to shift gears and prioritize domestic tourists. Local customers are less likely to cancel too, as they will only have to pay attention to local restrictions and are not as likely to have to quarantine after their visit.

STAYCATION

Staycation is another trend that gained popularity during the pandemic. It represents a holiday spent in one's home country or home rather than abroad. Often involves day trips for exploring local attractions and activities. This type of vacation is ideal for people who are feeling the need of escaping out of their homes but want to avoid the ongoing Covid-19 regulations.

GROWTH OF CONTACTLESS PAYMENTS

Contactless payments have been trending in tourism even before the pandemic, but the emergence of options like Google Pay, PhonePe, Paytm and Amazon Pay have helped to take this to the next level. Customers do not even need to carry around a debit card or credit card to pay for meals, hotel stays, transport, and other services. Allowing contactless payments has enabled tourism companies to reduce friction and improve the speed of check-ins and check-outs (Mirzaei, et. al. 2019). It also means goods can be paid for swiftly, encouraging spontaneous purchases. With coronavirus, contactless payments are in greater demand than ever, as staff and customers often prefer to avoid handling cash.

Voice Search & Voice Control

With home smart speakers growing in popularity, as well as mobile assistants like Siri, Alexa, Google Assistant and Bixby, more and more tourism customers are turning to voice search. For those in the tourism industry, it is important to capture these guests by structuring website content properly so it appears in voice search and allows for voice bookings.

Tourist information is a key part of the customer experience with many companies and voice control and AI can be invaluable here. Moreover, hotel rooms can include smart speakers or other IoT devices that are compatible with voice control, allowing users to more easily turn

VIRTUAL REALITY TOURISM TRENDS

Virtual reality is another of the major tourism trends. Through online VR tours, customers can experience hotel interiors, restaurant interiors, outdoor tourist attractions and more, all from their home. This technology can be very useful at the decision-making phase of the customer journey (Bec, et al, 2021). This can then be the difference between customers completing a booking or backing out. VR is especially useful within the context of COVID, where customers may have second thoughts and may need extra encouragement to press ahead with their plans.

ECO TRAVEL

Tourism trends are heavily influenced by the concerns and mores of the customer base. As a new generation becomes increasingly relevant in the marketplace, the ideals driving their purchasing decisions create new tourism trends. Eco travel is just one example of these tourism trends, reflecting a growing concern among today's travellers for ethical and sustainable tourism options. Eco travel includes simple changes, such as the availability of carbon credits when booking a flight or the option to rent an electric instead of a conventional vehicle. More sophisticated examples might include tourism with a volunteer element, perhaps working on a nature reserve or engaging in conservation work.

LOCAL EXPERIENCE

Today's tourists don't want to be insulated from the places they visit inside a cultural bubble. They want to engage with and participate in the local culture. From enjoying local cuisine to celebrating regional festivals and holidays, local experiences are set to become some of the top tourist trends to watch. One example of a popular local experience would be visiting Japan during a major festival, renting formal Japanese clothes to wear, consuming regional delicacies and engaging in traditional games or cultural activities. Another might be a long stay with a host family in the destination country as a means to learn more about the local culture.

PERSONALISATION

Personalisation can apply to every aspect of the tourist experience. Today's consumers expect experiences that closely match their personal preferences, from destinations to accommodation and the kinds of activities they engage in. The more closely an experience can be tailored to a client's desires and expectations, the more likely they are to return and to use the same service again.

ROBOTS, CHATBOTS AND AUTOMATION

Hotels have been installing interactive robots to handle certain reception duties or even having them serve food and drink to visitors. One of the more eye-catching examples of these particular tourism trends is Connie, the Hilton Hotel chain's robot concierge. Many customers now book their travel and accommodation with the help of internet chatbots, specifically tailored. AI who can handle queries and assist customers with useful information when human operators are unavailable.

ARTIFICIAL INTELLIGENCE

Artificial intelligence is becoming increasingly important to the tourism industry. Machine learning technology is now firmly entrenched in the marketing of the tourism sector, with AI helping to personalise the experience of finding and booking tours and trips. AI is also increasingly valuable in contexts such as smart hotel rooms, identifying the likely needs of guests and fine-tuning the environment and services to fit the guest's needs and preferences. Artificial intelligence is finding applications everywhere, from customer service to security. Future AI tourism trends to watch out for might include self-driving vehicles and virtual guides for tourism.

RECOGNITION TECHNOLOGY

Recognition technology is one of those increasingly important travel and tourism trends that's starting to creep into a multitude of different areas. One of the most familiar applications of recognition technology for a frequent traveller is the bank of automatic gates at some borders. The gates are capable of reading the data on the traveller's passport or ID card and matching it to their face using a camera and facial recognition technology. Recognition technology is one of the big tourism trends in the hospitality industry too, with voice recognition becoming more and more popular as a method of control in smart hotel rooms.

INTERNET OF THINGS (IOT)

IoT is relevant to many tourism trends. IoT devices are gadgets equipped with a microprocessor and some form of digital connectivity, allowing them to connect to, and be controlled from, the internet. IoT devices include heating and cooling systems, entertainment systems and other items often found in a hotel room, giving rise to "smart" hotel rooms. The IoT is also used to integrate services in a hospitality setting, for example by allowing guests to book activities (a session in the hotel's spa, swimming in the pool, training in the gym etc.) or request such things as room service or extra linen via a hub or a smartphone application.

AUGMENTED REALITY (AR)

Where VR simulates entire environments and experiences, augmented reality combines real-world experiences and virtual elements. A familiar example would be the smartphone game Pokémon Go, where imaginary creatures are superimposed on real-time footage of the player's environment. In the tourist industry, this is obviously very useful: instead of fantasy monsters. AR smartphone apps can show tourists information about the area they're exploring. This could be historical details about buildings and landmarks, or listings and menus for entertainment venues and local eateries. Museums make increasing use of AR, allowing visitors to view artefacts with their original appearance as a virtual overlay. Other augmented reality applications might include internet-enabled virtual maps.

HEALTHY AND ORGANIC FOOD

Healthy food and the kind of fare consumed by tourists used to be antonyms in the minds of many travellers, with holidays traditionally representing a chance to break one's diet and indulge in forbidden treats. Today's travellers know that delicious and nutritious food are not exclusive concepts. The organic food movement is also affecting tourism trends, with more eateries and hotels offering organic options.

CONCLUSION:

Travelling has been a common passion for many, for decades, be it for leisure or business. Even in a downturn, when the volumes might dip, the travel sector has seldom faced total lockdown of operations, let alone for months at a stretch. The COVID-19 crisis has conjured up one such rare situation for the travel industry and is probably the worst hit by the pandemic. At the same time, the COVID-19 crisis has a Pandora's box of important learnings that the travel industry can draw from. While the tourism industry will take some time to recover from the severe impact of the pandemic, the lessons imbibed from Covid pandemic will help the industry to meet the new requirement of consumers. It is also quite obvious that tomorrow's tourists and tour operators will tend to rely more on technology. The adoption of the latest technological advancement will be a game changer for tourism players to stay ahead of competition.

REFERENCES:

➤ Abbas, J., Mubeen, R., Iorember, P. T., Raza, S., & Mamirkulova, G. (2021). Exploring the impact of COVID-19 on tourism: transformational potential and implications for a sustainable recovery of the travel and leisure industry. *Current Research in Behavioral Sciences, 2, 100033.*

➤ Bec, A., Moyle, B., Schaffer, V., Timms, K., (2021). Virtual reality and mixed reality for second chance tourism. Tourism Management, 83, 104256.

➤ Cohen, S.A., Prayag, G. and Moital, M. (2013), Consumer behavior in tourism: concepts, influences and opportunities, *Current Issues in Tourism*, 17 (10), 872-909.

➤ Mirzaei, R., Sadin, M. and Pedram, M. (2021), Tourism and COVID-19: changes in travel patterns and tourists' behavior in Iran, *Journal of Tourism Futures*,

➤ Sharma, G. D., Thomas, A., & Paul, J. (2021). Reviving tourism industry post-COVID-19: A resilience-based framework. *Tourism Management Perspectives*, 37, 100786.

➤ Yang, Y., Zhang, H. and Chen, X. (2020), Coronavirus pandemic and tourism: dynamic stochastic general equilibrium modeling of infectious disease outbreak, *Annals of Tourism Research*, 83, 102913.

CHAPTER 12

INTERNATIONAL TOURISTS IN KERALA –PROSPECTS AND PROBLEMS

Ms. Jisny K.E,
Post Graduate student,
Department of Home Science
St. Teresa's College, Kerala, India

Smt Teresa Kuncheria
Associate Professor,
Department of Home Science
St. Teresa's College, Kerala, India

ABSTRACT

Tourism is one of the fastest growing industries in the world. Tourism industry brings in much revenue to the state of Kerala, and any industry, if it has to be sustained, needs to be analyzed for its opportunities and challenges. The study aims at ascertaining the profile of international tourists visiting Kerala, understand their preferences pertaining to destination, food, stay and travel and reasons contributing to dissatisfaction if any. The method selected for study was a survey. Hundred International tourists were purposively selected for the study and information collected with the help of an interview schedule. The results revealed that majority of the tourists were coming from UK, USA and Canada. From Asian countries (China, Japan, South Korea) the number of tourists were very less. Many have visited Kerala more than twice. Majority came with leisure/ entertainment as their main purpose of visit, only a few came for medical /educational / business purposes. The destinations most preferred by the tourists were beaches and historically significant places. They spent a substantial amount of money on products and services from Kerala. Safety and transportation facilities were recognized as good, while lack of cleanliness was a cause of concern. Though some of the tourists felt that most goods and services were highly priced and money transactions were quite difficult, many expressed high levels of satisfaction from their visit to Kerala.

Key words: Tourism, International tourists, Prospects, Problems.

INTRODUCTION

India is one of the greatest tourist destinations due its rich and varied heritage and culture. Globally, India is seen as a land of diverse climatic and scenic beauty and a plethora of ecological features that are of interest to any traveler. Statistics reveal that a large number of foreigners are seeking out Indian destinations (Chauhan, 2010).

According to WTTC (2015), tourism contributes 10 % of the global GDP, 7% of the total world exports, 30 % of services exports and 9.09% global employment while in India the contribution of tourism to GDP has been 4.90%, thus accounting for around 6.78 % of the total employment in the country. Manoj (2010) also affirms that tourism is a major contributor to the national GDP and creates much opportunities for employment.The average share of generation of employment through tourism in India is more than the global average. World Travel and Tourism reports throws light on the fact that 9.6 % of GDP during 2016 was generated from tourism. It has led to the generation of 40.343 million jobs amounting to 9.3% of the total employment (Sumaira, 2018). Tourism is noted as the third highest foreign exchange earner (Chokalingam, 2010).

Dharmarajan (1999) opines that an important aspect of the tourism industry was that it could be made more sustainable so as to alleviate poverty and ensure better standards of living among the people, especially those in the rural areas. Sinha (2006) notes that as per records, 12 countries around the world are living in abject poverty with less than a dollar per day for their sustenance and out of these, eleven countries gain their significant revenue from tourism. (Sinha, 2006).

The number of tourists from the Eastern regions of the world were less when compared with those of the West with only 13 % in 2008. Among the Eastern countries, it was seen that Japanese and the Koreans made up to 3 and 2.29 % respectively of the total number of tourists who visited (Chowdhary 2011).

The data regarding the number of tourists who visited Kerala during the year 2018 was 109187, with a variation/ increase of 0.42 % over the previous year. The revenue earned is to a tune of 8764 crores with an increase in 4.4 % over the previous year (Abraham, 2018).Manoj (2010) notes that Kerala is a much favoured destination for many due to the varied ecology, ranging from mountains to backwaters and diverse flora and fauna.

Kerala has been listed as one of the ten paradises of the world, by National Geographic. This has catapulted Kerala into one of the most desirable places on the traveller's map. This coastal paradise is called God's own Country, due to its rich greenery and exquisite locations. Moreover the culture and tradition of Kerala, with its varied art forms like Kathakali, Mohiniyattam, etc and the numerous temples offers a plethora of experiences to those who visit here. Ayurveda is another strong point which brings in a vast number of tourists – for self-rejuvenation and also for heath treatments. Medical tourism, is also a new arena which is opened due to the availability of numerous expert doctors in various fields and also the availability of multi facility hospitals with avenues for world class surgical facilities.The Kerala cuisine is also a whole new experience.Ranging from traditional sweets and savouries to sea food delicacies,Kerala can be a treasure house of taste and aroma- cloves, pepper and cardamom are the main crops of this region.

MATERIALS AND METHODS

The objectives of the study were to ascertain the profile of International Tourists visiting Kerala, to understand their travel details, purpose and duration of visit. The preferences of the tourists pertaining to destinations, food, stay and travel were also studied and so were the problems they faced during their stay in Kerala. The method selected for study was a survey, and with an interview schedule, data was collected from 100 international tourists selected purposively from Ernakulam district.

RESULTS AND DISCUSSION

The results of the study revealed the following

Table 1 Demographic profile of International tourists

Particulars	Options	Percentage
Age	• Below 25 years	48

	• 25-45 years	34
	• 45-65 years	16
	• Above 65 years	2
Gender	• Female	61
	• Male	39
Occupation	• Working	94
	• Non- working	6

Forty eight percent of the respondents were below 25 years of age, and 34 % in the age group of 25 to 45 years. Only 2% were above 65 years. Sixty one respondents were females and thirty nine respondents were males. Majority (94%) of the respondents wereworking, (out of which 42% of the respondents were students who under took various jobs). Non- working individuals were only 6%.

COUNTRY OF RESIDENCE

International Tourists came from various destinations to Kerala. Tourists who came from European countries (United kingdom, Scotland, Poland, Holland, France, Germany, Spain, Switzerland, Austria, Belgium, Ireland, Italy, Sweden) were (66%), Canada(12%) and USA (19%). From Asian countries (China, Japan, South Korea) the number of tourists were only 3 percent of the total respondents.

Fig 1   Country of residence

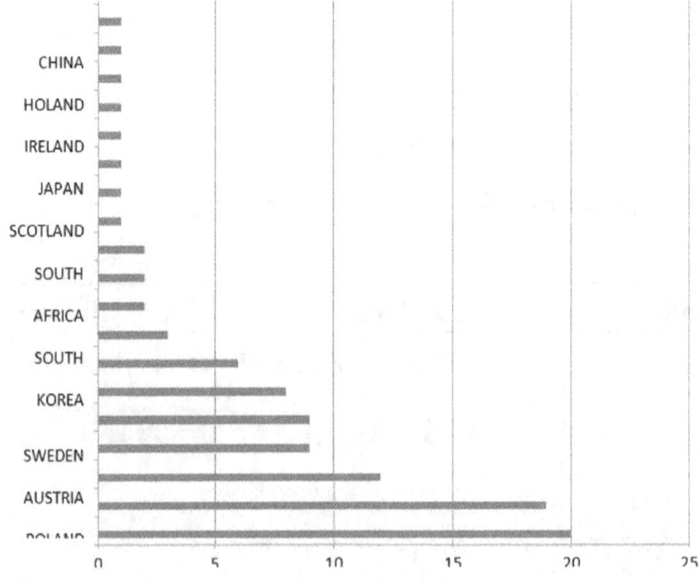

Uk-20, Usa-19, Canada- 12, Germany- 6, Australia-8, Poland-1, SouthKorea-1 , Japan-1, Italy-9, France-9, Austria-2, Scotland-1, Spain-3,Sweden-1, Belgium-1,South Africa-1, Ireland-1, Switerzerland-2,China-1, Holland-1.

TRAVEL DETAILS OF THE RESPONDENTS

International tourists relied on various sources of information to choose their destination. It was found that around 37% of respondents relied on information from relatives/friends, 33% relied on the internet and 10% on travel magazines. It was interesting to note that only 6% relied on travel agencies and very few relied on advertisements (2%).

Fig 2: Most relied source of information

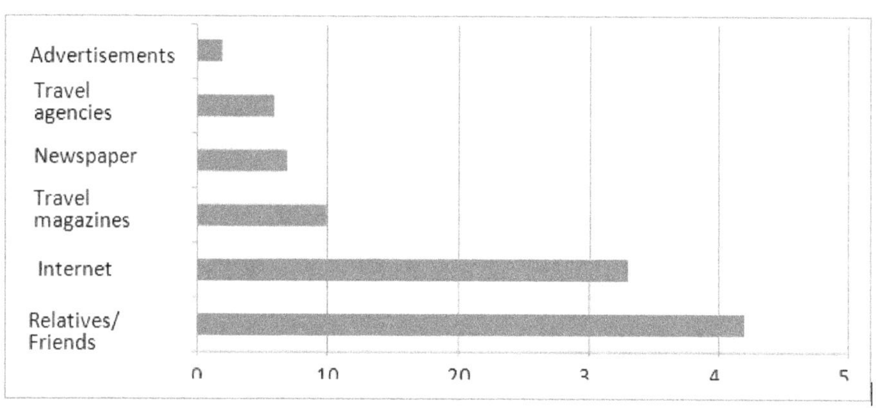

NATURE OF TRAVEL ARRANGEMENTS

It was seen that majority of the respondents (72 %) booked their travel arrangements by themselves while 28% of the respondents booked through agencies.

MAIN PURPOSE OF VISIT

Tourists came from different destinations, for fulfilling various needs. From the study itwas seen that majority of the tourists came with leisure/ entertainment as their main purpose of visit (87%). Among them, most were interested in learning the culture of theland (37%), the environment (28%), the adventure it offered (16%) and 6 % were interested in its historical significance. A few (7 %) came for medical reasons, a lesser number came as part of educational purposes (5%) and only 1% for business purpose.

FREQUENCY AND DURATION OF VISIT

It was seen that more than half the tourists (67 %) were visiting Kerala for the first time,while 14 % have visited twice. It is interesting to note that 19% of tourists have visited Kerala more than twice. The reasons stated were - the beautiful destinations, their interest in the tradition and food of Kerala. While conducting the survey, many of the tourists commented positively about Kerala's richculture, vibrant lifestyle and hospitality

More than three quarters (78%) of the respondents have stayed for more than a week. A minority (9 %) have stayed for an extended period of time. Many chose to see the ongoingfestivals and have stayed upto 15 days.

Table II   Type of accommodation

Particulars	Percentage
Hotels /resorts	61
Home stay	25
Family residences	14

Most of the respondents stayed at hotels/resorts (61%)while 25 % preferred home stays. Fourteen percent were staying at family residences with people who were known to them.

PARTNER OF TRAVEL

The study showed that 46% of international tourists visited with their families, 31 % came along with a group, 28% came with friends, and 13% travelled alone. In this study,all those who travelled alone were men.

TRAVEL GUIDE SERVICES AVAILED

It was seen that travel guide services were relied upon at certain times only by 39 percentof the tourists, while 28 percent availed it always.

Table III   Most preferred destination in Kerala

Particulars	Percentage
Back waters	21
Beaches	32
Commercially busy cities	10
Hill stations	15
Historically significant places	22

For most of the International tourists, beaches were the most preferred destination (32%), followed by historically significant places (22 %) and backwaters (21 %), while others selected hill stations (15%), and only a minority preferred commercially busycities (10%).

OPINION REGARDING FACILITIES OFFERED AT TOURIST DESTINATIONS

Tourists are very keen in observing the facilities offered at different destinations. Understanding the lack of facilities as pointed out by tourists would be helpful in makingtravel destinations more suitable and perfect. Hence responses were sought from the tourists regarding safety, cleanliness, transport facilities to and fro from the selected destination, food facilities and rest/leisure services provided at these destinations.

Table IV Opinion regarding facilities offered at tourist destinations

Particulars	Good	Fair	Poor
Cleanliness	25	33	42
Food facilities	53	37	10
Rest/Leisure facilities	38	53	9
Safety	48	42	10
Transportation	46	40	14

Nearly half the respondents felt that safety (48%) and transportation services (46%) at most places were good. However, poor scores were given by nearly half the respondents (42%) with regard to cleanliness. Many pointed out that there were many areas which were polluted with wasteespecially plastic products, and lack of cleanliness, unavailability of trash bins, dumping of commercial and domestic waste in the road sides were a cause of concern.

DETAILS PERTAINING TO FOOD AND TRANSPORT SERVICES AVAILED

Many international tourists were interested in the varied types of food available in theland. They also exhibited much interest in various modes of transport.With regard to food, it was seen that 63% preferred to try out traditional Kerala cuisine,while 31% retained their own food preferences.

With regard to transport, tourists availed different modes of transport when they were in Kerala. With regards to their most preferred mode of transport, it was seen that 59% preferred travelling by car, 23 % preferred buses, 17 % preferred auto rickshaws, while a minority (1%) travelled by cycle.

AVERAGE EXPENDITURE ON PRODUCTS AND SERVICES FROM KERALA

The average amount spent by tourists on products and services from Kerala, other than that spent on basic travel, accommodation and food were studied. This brings in extra revenue to the localites. It was seen that more than half the respondents (55 %) spent an extra amount ranging from Rs 10,000 to 50,000, 29 % spent more than Rs 50,000 and

16 % spent below Rs 10,000 on products and services from Kerala.

International tourists in India also faced problems during their stay. Many faced language difficulties (79%) mainly related to pronunciation and slang, rather than the lack of knowledge of the language.

A large number of tourists (60%) felt that most goods and services were highly priced here, when compared to different parts of India and the world, 38 % also felt that there was no consistency in the services provided to tourists. While some areas catered very well for tourists, some areas provided only meagre facilities.

They also felt that services were also not consistent with the amount of money paid for it. A few tourists (19%) felt that money transactions were very difficult for them. One of the major problems faced by tourists was that many shops did not accept international cards.

Fig – 3 Most challenging problem faced by tourists

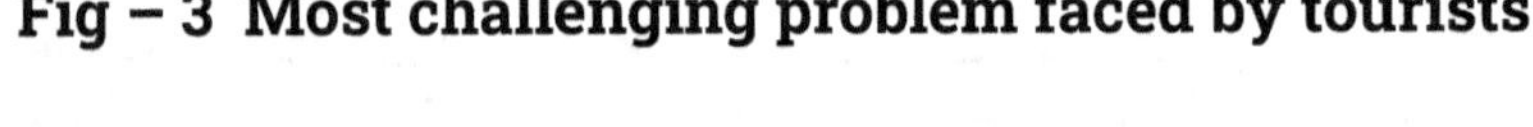

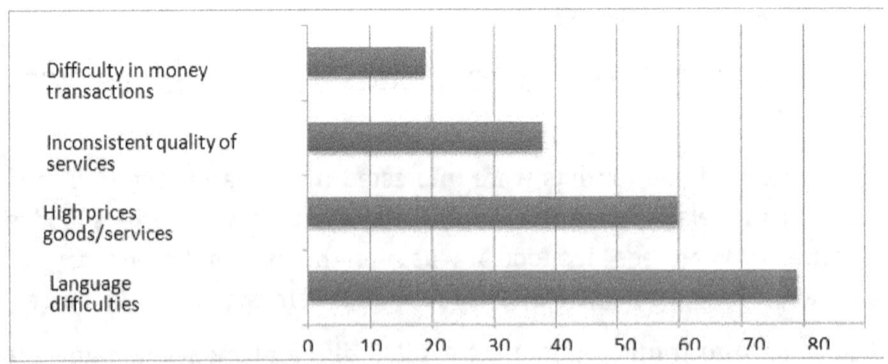

OVERALL SATISFACTION REGARDING VISIT TO KERALA

Tourists were asked their opinion regarding overall satisfaction of their visit to Kerala. Out of the respondents, 38 % felt it was excellent, 43 % felt that it was very good. Aminority (4%) rated it as average, none rated it as poor.

Fig -4   Overall satisfaction regarding visit to Kerala

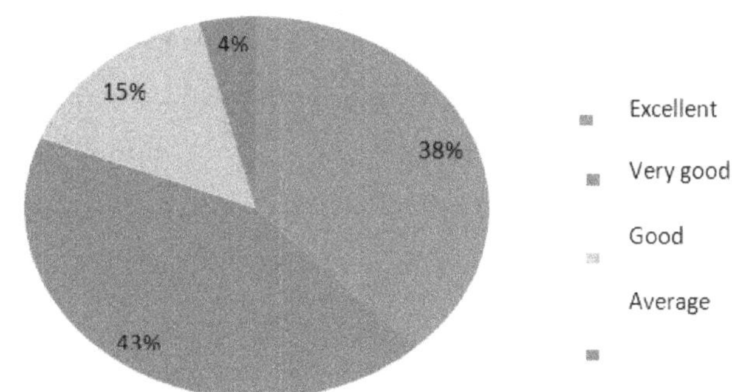

CONCLUSION

Kerala is known for its varied destinations and it attracts many tourists from around the world. Majority of the tourists were from UK, USA and Canada. From Asian countries (China, Japan, South Korea) the number of tourists were very less. Many have visited Kerala more than twice. Majority came with leisure/entertainment as their main purpose of visit, only a few came for medical / educational/ business purposes. They spent a substantial amount of money here on products and services. Safety and transportation facilities were recognized as good, while lack of cleanliness was a cause of concern. Tourists felt that most goods and services were highly priced here, when compared to other parts in India and felt that money transaction were difficult.

REFERENCES

➤ Chauhan, (2010). Analyzing tourism potential of Tamil Nadu state of India: A people – tourist's perception approach. Journal of environmental research and development, Vol.5, No.2

➤ Madhavi Chokalingam, (2010). Problems encountered by tourists. Department of

Business Administration. Annamalai University India- Vol.3

➤ Abraham Rajesh, (2018). Kerala Government's claim on its tourism sector isinflated. Express News Service.

➤ Chowdhary Samit, (2011). Tourist inflow to India from East Asian Countriesstudy of trend and pattern. University of Assam, Department of Business Administration

➤ Dharmarajan, (1999). Tourism - An Instrument for development. Yojana Vol.3, No.8. Lakshmi Nair, Dhanuraj (2018). Kerala Tourism – The role of government and Economic Impacts. Centre for public research.

➤ Madhavi Chokalingam, (2010). Problems encountered by tourists. Department of Business Administration. Annamalai University India- Vol.3.

➤ Manoj, (2010). Tourism in Kerala, a case study of the imperatives and impediments with focus on eco- tourism. Cochin University Science andTechnology.

➤ Nazar Abdul (2018). Tourism in Kerala, an evaluate study. Mahatma Gandhi University.

➤ Sinha, (2006). Global tourism, Sustainable tourism, and Eco tourism. Code of ethics, charts and guidelines, resolutions. SBS publishers and distributions of Pvt. Ltd, New Delhi.Sumaira, (2018). Issues and challenges faced by tourism sector of Kashmir – Aconceptual study. Assistant professor, Department of management studies, University of Kashmir.

➤ https://wttc.org/News-Article/New-report-from-WTTC-and-Trip-com-Group-reveals-latest-consumer-trends-and-the-shift-in-traveller-behaviours

➤ https://www.unwto.org>publication.

CHAPTER 13

A STUDY ON BEACH TOURISM IN THIRUVANANTHAPURAM DISTRICT

Sumi John
Research Scholar, Department of Commerce
University of Kerala

ABSTRACT

Beach tourism is an ongoing sector in Thiruvananthapuram district due to its wider acceptability among domestic and foreign touristers Various subsidiary businesses that grow along the beach tourism are local home stays for foreigners, restorts, local arts and crafts etc. Big Business firms are always showing interest in investing in beach tourism and this can be confirmed by the rising number of beach hotels and restaurants in and around various beaches in Trivandrum. Varkala, Kovalam, Shangumugham, Veli etc are some of the key seashores that attract a number of visitors every single day. Some of the beaches are located very next to some pilgrimage centres such as vettukad church, Sree Narayana samadhi in Varkala which also attracts many visitors. Local Street vendors' businesses are progressing because the visitors are likely to buy crafts and attractive pieces which are made out of sea shells to keep them as a memory of their visit.

Keywords: Beach tourism, Sea erosion

INTRODUCTION

Beach tourism is defined as "it is a travel for recreation, leisure or business purposes specifically on beaches. Beach tourism is one of the fastest growing industries. It supports overall development of the economy by increasing the foreign exchanges. Food industry and travel industry also grow and prosper beyond the border of the country in the light of beach tourism. Beaches are adjoined with resorts, food stalls, playgrounds, parks, car and bus parking areas, hotels etc, to retain and attract the foreigners. Kerala is a fabulous state with wider availability of natural resources and wonderful locations seemed to be an attractive destination for tourists. The state has around 550km long coastlines, with amazing holiday spots. Thiruvananthapuram or Trivandrum is Kerala's southernmost district, having approximately 78 km of shoreline along the Arabian Sea on the west (8° 17' 35"N–8° 51' 45"N latitudes and 76° 40' 23"E–77° 17' 2" E longitudes) (Rejith et al., 2020).it is the capital city of Kerala. There are around eleven beaches in the district. The beaches act as a perfect place for social interaction and economic events. The natives of the district spend their leisure time with their family and friends and an ideal holiday destination. It creates a lot of job opportunities for the society. Street sellers are active there for selling a variety of products. Street foods are sold at the seashore. It indicates the culture of our locality. The areas surrounding the beach area are fully developed due to economic flow of wealth from higher income people to underdeveloped sections.

REVIEW OF LITERATURE

Dr Ezreth P(2019) the study focused on environmental problems faced by Kovalam beach in thiruvananthapuram district. It is a perfect place for foreigners with well established resorts, ayurvedic treatment, sunbath etc. The coastal areas are not maintained properly due to intense human presence and inefficiency of higher authorities.

Sachin pavithran et.al (2014) this study investigates various coastal issues in kerala. It includes sand mining, development of ports and harbor, construction of luxury hotels, house boats, swimming pools, coastal erosion etc. Heavy rain and changing weather conditions erode the seashore environment and it becomes difficult to recover to the original form.

Lakshmi S R(2015) the study is about the impact of tourism development in coastal areas of papanasam beach in varkala. Industrialization, urbanization and commercialization are the reasons behind the detorization of the coastal environment. Dr A Nishad (2019) the travel industry seems to be one of the fastest growing industries and increasing foreign exchange in our country. It is not a distinct concept; it includes so many areas of operations. The tourism focused on unity and harmony among the nations. It involves a monetary movement of services and is unique in nature.

IMPORTANCE OF THE STUDY

The tourism industry is a milestone for the modern economy. Tourism is considered to be a marketing product in our country. People travel from place to another to watch something new and experience something which is different such as a variety of food, places, environment, ecosystem etc. It creates a lot of employment opportunities for every sector of the economy. There are different types of tourism such as food tourism, coastal tourism, agriculture tourism, eco tourism, educational tourism, dark tourism, sustainable tourism etc. tourism promote unity and harmony among the nations. It helps to transfer social culture beyond the borders. It helps to increase the foreign reserve of the country. So it is important to study the present situation of beaches in the district.

STATEMENT OF THE PROBLEM

Tourism plays an important role in the overall development of the society. Beach tourism not only includes the blue sea with blue tidal waves, but also infrastructural facilities that are meant for leisure and entertainment that attract the attention of a single person. Beaches consist of ocean ecosystems along with its surrounding natural resources . Thiruvananthapuram district is blessed with a lot of beaches with a variety of amenities. Today the situation is different due to Covid epidemic and heavy rain. The flow of foreigners is too low. In some situations entry to the beaches are prohibited due to violent seashores.

OBJECTIVES

1. To study the present situation of beach tourism in thiruvananthapuram districts

2. To study the satisfaction of people in thiruvananthapuram towards beach tourism.

BEACHES IN THIRUVANANTHAPURAM

1. Kovalam beach : Kovalam is an international beach with three adjacent beaches. It is 16km away from thiruvananthapuram district. It is famous for private resorts, health resorts, shopping zones, swimming pools, yoga, ayurvedic massage centers, sunbathing, herbal body toning massages, special cultural programmes etc. The shoreline of Kovalam is referred to as "heaven of the south".

2. Shankumugham Beach : Shankumugham beach has a vast spread of white sand with wonderful shorelines and has a wider horizon which separates sea and sky. The other attraction is the"matsyakanyaka" , a 35meter long mermaid figure constructed near the shoreline. The"old coffee house" is the restaurant parallel to the sea, which provides seafood and tasty dishes. Today this beach lost its beauty and was completely closed due to sea erosion. The shoreline completely disappeared due to sea overload of water. The heavy tidal waves destroy the public amenities close to the sea.

3. Veli : Veli beach is merely 12km away from Trivandrum city. Thechildren park and garden is the biggest attraction in this area. The veli tourist village is the place where veli lake meets the Arabian sea. A floating café run by Kerala tourism development corporation (KTDC) is an attractive spot. The country's first solar energy driven miniature train is opened for tourists by the government.

4. Vizhinjam : The beach is around 15 km away from Trivandrum city. It is famous for saagarika vizhinjam marine aquarium and rock cut temple of lord shiva with goddess parvati near the beach. The vizhinjam international deepwater multipurpose seaport also called vizhinjam port is under construction. After construction it will become the deepest port in india. So after that it will become an important destination for tourists.

5. Varkala beach : It is 51km away to the north of Trivandrum city. The separate beach, which is 10km away from varkala is renowned for a natural spring called papanasam beach. The other attractions of these destinations are 200years old Janardhana swamy temple and Sree Naryana guru's sivagiri mutt.

RESEARCH METHODOLOGY

This study follows descriptive research design.

SOURCES OF DATA

Primary data

The primary data were collected through direct observation method and questionnaire method. Questionnaire was prepared and circulated among respondents interview schedules were for conducting interviews. Questionnaire is divided into two parts, the first part includes the demographic information about the respondents. The second part includes factors that determine the satisfaction level of the respondents towards beach tourism in thiruvananthapuram district.

Secondary data

The secondary sources include journals, reports, presentations, documents, books, handouts, websites, published and unpublished articles related to similar areas.

SAMPLE SIZE

The universe of the study was the domestic customers from Trivandrum district, who always visit the beach on a regular basis. The sample consists of 50 respondents. Simple random sampling method is used for selecting sample size.

TOOLS FOR DATA ANALYSIS

The statistical tools such as percentage and mean score were used for analyzing the data.

DATA ANALYSIS AND INTERPRETATIONS

Table -1: shows demographic profile of touristers

Demographic factors		Number of respondents	percentage
Gender	Male	32	64
	Female	18	36
	Total	50	100
Age Group	Less than 20 years	16	32
	21-35 years	19	38
	36-50years	5	10
	50-65 years	6	12
	Above 65 years	4	8
	Total	50	100
Marital status	Married	29	58
	Unmarried	21	42
	Total	50	100

Educational qualification	SSLC	5	15
	Higher secondary	3	6
	Graduation	14	28
	Post graduation	12	24
	Professional degree	11	22
	Others	4	16
	Total	50	100
Occupation	Govt employee	27	54
	Private job	12	24
	Business	5	10
	Agriculture	2	4
	Others	4	8
	Total	50	100
Interested beach	Kovalam	21	42
	Shanghumugham	2	4
	Veli	16	32
	Vizhinjam	8	16
	Others	3	6
	Total	50	100

Interpretation: out of 50 respondents, 32 males and 18 females are selected.

More people visit the beaches from the age group of 20-35 years.58% of the people spend their leisure time at the beach with their family. Most of them are highly qualified people. From the data we can analyse that government employees often visit the beach. Majority of them consider Kovalam as the best beach in Thiruvananthapuram district.

Table 2: shows the factors which determine the satisfaction level of the people towards beach tourism

Satisfaction factors	Strongly agree	Agree	Neutral	Dis-agree	Strongly disagree	Total score	Mean score
Sanitary and cleanliness	15	60	66	12	4	157	3.14
Food and beverages	60	56	36	14	5	171	3.42
Accommodation	45	84	36	14	1	180	3.6
Parking facilities	160	40	18	4	0	222	4.44
Scenic beauty	120	64	15	10	0	209	4.18
Entertainment activities	25	72	36	18	6	157	3.14
Health treatments	170	48	12	0	0	230	4.6
Security measures	60	60	36	12	5	173	3.46
Travelling facilities	165	60	6	0	0	231	4.62
Leisure and recreational activities	55	72	45	8	2	182	3.64

Interpretation:- Domestic consumers of beach tourism were satisfied with parking facilities and travelling facilities in the beach area. But less satisfied with sanitary and cleanliness. The people want good waste management arrangements in the areas. They also give weight age to health treatment and security measures.

FINDINGS

➤ It is been found that the domestic touristers are satisfied with scenic travelling facilities and parking facilities in the beaches

➤ The health treatment in case of any emergency is provided in every beaches

➤ There is a poor waste management facilities in the beaches

➤ In some beaches there is a lack of entertainment activities in the beaches to attract the tourists

SUGGESTIONS

➤ More advertisements and promotional measures are needed to attract a lot foreign tourister in our country

➤ Avoid overexploitation of natural resources in beaches

➤ Natural friendly infrastructural facilities must be developed, by allocating government funds to make tourism a big success.

➤ Avoid unscientific construction activities around the seashore

CONCLUSION

Kerala is located between western ghats mountain range on the east and the Arabian sea on the west. It is famous for coastal tourism and its natural environment. Thiruvananthapuram is well known for beaches and its scenic beauty. This study is based on the present situation of beaches in our areas. Industrialization and urbanization contributes to a lot of changes in beach tourism. But the situation is more pathetic and intolerable due to heavy monsoon rain and sea erosion. Some beach areas are totally destroyed and lost their beauty but are still waiting for renewal . It is the responsibility of the higher authorities to nourish tourism in its most possible way.. Foreigners are the people who respect our society and spread our culture across the countries.so treating them with good amenities is more important than anything else in this world.

BIBLIOGRAPHY

➤ Malhotra, R.K. (2005). Tourism Planning and Management. Anmol Publications Pvt. Ltd. New Delhi. p332.

➤ Nishad, A. (2019). A STUDY ON BEACH TOURISM AND ITS OVERALL DISTRICT DEVELOPMENT – A SPECIAL REFERENCE TO BEACHES IN TRIVANDRUM D. International Journal of Advance and Innovative Research, 6(2), 1–7

➤ Reshma sandeep kumar Dey et.al. (2021). SOLASTALGIA INSIGHTS FROM YOUNG TOURISTS- A STUDY WITH REFERENCE TO SHANGHUMUGHAM BEACH, KERALA. Sambodhi(ugc care journal). Vol-44, no-01(xvi), pg 68-75

➤ Lakshmi S R, et al.(2016). TRANSFORMATION OF COASTAL SETTLEMENT DUE

TO TOURISM. Procedia technology, vol 24, pg 1668-1680

➤ Dr Ezreth P. (2019). ENVIRONMENTAL PROBLEMS FACED BY KOVALAM BEACH. International journal of social relevance & concern, vol 7, pg 1-5

➤ Sachin pavithran. A.P et.al(2014). AN ANALYSIS OF VARIOUS COASTAL ISSUES IN KERALA. International journal of scientific research and education, vol2, pg 1993-2001

CHAPTER 14

ROLE OF TRAVEL INFLUENCERS IN TOURISM INDUSTRY

Ms. Jeena Joy
Research Scholar,
Mahatma Gandhi University Kottayam

ABSTRACT

The growth of social media leads to the development of different industries. Tourism is one of the industries which is benefited from social media developments. Travel influencers are a new phenomenon in the tourism industry which is currently connecting with consumers through various social media platforms like face book, Instagram, you tube etc. This article tries to identify the emerging role of travel influencers in the tourism industry.

Keywords: Tourism industry, Influencer marketing, Social Media Influencers, Travel Influencer.

INTRODUCTION

Tourism is a process of travelling away from usual surroundings for a pleasure, relaxation and leisure. Tourism is an industry which contributes to the economic and social development of a nation. The development of technology and growth of social media have made a positive impact on tourism industry. Nowadays people who are wish to travel always prefer social media platforms for location search and sharing travel experiences. Tour companies are now focusing on social media marketing in order to attract and inspire people to make a travel. Social media marketing means the marketing of products and services through various social media platforms like Face book, Instagram, you tube etc. The emergence of influencers in social media creates a drastic change in the behaviour of common people. Social media influencers also called as social media celebrities. They are people who prove their talents on a particular niche and have an expertise on specific fields. People who have similar taste or interest wish to follow these celebrities through their social media channels in order to seek knowledge and advices. But some people follow these social media celebrities for an entertainment. Whatever be the reason these influencers are gaining more popularity among the society.

Marketing is an area which always focuses on innovations in order attract consumers. Marketers on different industries are now focusing on developing new marketing platforms for this digital era. Social media marketing is found as one of the successful marketing strategies implemented by modern marketers. Tourism is one of the industries which successfully utilizing this marketing strategy. The growth of different travel influencers in social media brings a positive impact on travel consumers. Travel influencers are people who make travelling to various destinations and share their travelling experiences with their followers. The travel experiences of these influencers make an inspiration among their followers to conduct a trip to a same or similar place. Tourist companies are now focusing on this behavioural change of people and they make sponsorships to these travel influencers as part of the promotion of their tourist company. This article is focusing on the impact of travel influencers on tourism industry.

LITERATURE REVIEW

Kshitij Mokhare, Atul Satpuli, Vaibhav Pal, Prajakta Badwaik (2021): The study aims to explore various theories and studies to analyze the motives behind people to travel. It considered the attitude of young people towards travelling. The study reveals that influencer marketing holds a major role in influencing people to search for travel information and conduct travelling especially among young people.

Puta Gede Iwan Trisna Jaya, Ida Bagus Teddy Privanthara (2020) : This is an international study conducted at Bedugul, Indonesia. The study focuses on three variables such as brand image, social media influencers, destination image and their impact on purchase intension of foreign tourists. The study explores that all the three variables had a positive impact on purchase intension. The results of the study were verified through SEM analysis.

Ruby Andrew (2014): Social medias has a greater impact on travel decisions of consumers. Among the three popular media websites such as face book, you tube, and twitter, face book is considered as more relevant in influencing and attracting travel consumers.

Rebekha Anna Pop, Zsuzsa Saplacan, Dan Cristian, Dabija and Monika Anetta Alt (2021): The study focuses on how the variable called 'trust' on social media influencers affects the travel decision making process of consumers. The results of the study proves that trust of consumers on social media influencers (SMI) has a positive impact on every stage of their travel decision making. SMI are considered as a powerful marketing tool to attract travel consumers by tourism mareters.

Payal S Kapoor, M.S Balaji, Yang yang Jiang, Charles Jebarajakirthy (2021): The study explores the effectiveness of social media influencers. Two important variables considered for the study include argument quality and sponsorship status. The results of the study revealed that an attribute value message is more influenced in perceptions and intension of travel consumers.

Linh Hale, Hancer Murat (2021): The study is conducted to identify the impact of three variables called perceived attractiveness, trustworthiness and expertise on behavioural changes of viewers of travel vloggers on You tube. The findings reveals that all these three variables had positive influence on the viewers. And female vloggers are more attractive than male vloggers but credibility lies more on male vloggers. It is required to select a most appropriate travel vlogger in order to promote travel industry through social media platforms.

METHODOLOGY

This is a descriptive paper. The data for this paper is collected from secondary sources such as research articles, books, journals and websites.

TRAVEL INFLUENCERS IN TOURISM INDUSTRY

Travel Influencer

Travel influencers are those people who make travelling through different parts of the world and make videos of the same and share these videos and their travelling experiences in their social media channels. They always try to create a live experience with their followers throughout their travelling. Majority of their followers were travel lovers and these videos of influencers creates some kind of inspiration and enjoyment for them. Trust on these influencers by their followers is the major reason behind the growth of travel influencers in the world.

As a part of influencer marketing tourist companies, travel agencies, airlines will commit a partnership with most popular travel influencers in order to promote their business. As per the latest report 66% of marketers increased their investment in influencer marketing. Tourism marketers agreed that investment in influencer marketing is the most successful marketing strategy for this era.

TYPES OF TRAVEL INFLUENCERS

Solo Travel Influencer

Solo travelers are those who travel alone. They frequently share photos and vlogs from their travels. Influencers that promote solo travel generally work with a variety of brands while promoting the idea of solo travel. They usually advocate backpacking and offer suggestions for things to do as a solitary traveler. In the previous few years, the number of solo journeys has increased by roughly 80%, which is why solo traveler influencers are now in high demand.

Family travel Influencer

Family travel influencers are those people who travel along with their family members and share their travel journey through their social media channel. These influencers are focusing on to inspire their followers to make a family trip. The content and videos shared by family travelers include all details of their traveled destination which helps their followers to decide a suitable destination for a family trip.

Couple travel influencer

Newly married couples and those who plan for a honeymoon are inspired by of these influencers. Couple influencers share the details of destinations and the facilities offered there which gives a clear picture about that particular place. Today travel agencies are entering into contract with couple influencers to promote their special packages and to attract more consumers. The genuine reviews made by influencers increases their follower base.

Budget travel influencer

Budget travel influencers are focusing on cost less journeys. Majority of travel lovers are concern about their budget while planning a trip. People always make searches to find out a destination which satisfies their expectations and comes under their budget. Budget travel influencers are works on the social platform by promoting traveling with a planned budget. They also sometimes provide certain tips to minimize budget.

Religious travel Influencer

These are travelers whose major destinations include different religious places. They are influencing people who like to know about the history of religious places and who wish to visit such places. Religious travelers often help in increasing the number tourists to such religious areas.

FACTORS AFFECTING INFLUENCER MARKETING

The growth social media brings wide changes in the behaviour of consumers. The success of influencer marketing depends on many factors. All studies conducted in this field shows that trust is the most important factor behind a successful influencer marketing.

Trust

The success of influencer marketing depends on the trust of consumers towards influencers. A recent study states that today people have more trust on influencers than celebrities. If anyone lost their trust on influencers then they will unfollow them. So that influencers always try to provide authentic and useful information in order to keep their follower base.

Credibility

Credibility of the message shared by influencers have greater impact on influencer marketing. If anyone identifies a wrong information is shared by an influencer then he has the right to file suit against that influencer who shared the message. And if any loss incurred for his/her followers due to following influencer's information then as per legal provisions of the nation it the duty of the influencer to meet such losses. While sharing information through social medias influencers should have surety about the authenticity of their messages.

Attractiveness

The success of every marketing is based on the attractiveness of the content presented. Influencers on social media always tries to create attractive contents for their followers. The attractive presentation of influencers increases the number of followers which helps in the promotion of various products and services through influencer marketing.

Homophily

Homophily means the tendency of people to seek out to those who are similar to themselves. Influencer marketing is gaining popularity due the homophily nature of consumers. People always interested to listen to others who think and behave like themselves. That's why people who wish to travel likes to follow travel influencers.

Expertise

Influencers on a particular niche are basically expertise on that area. They create and share valuable and reliable messages to their followers through social media. Nowadays its common to seek suggestions from influencers by their followers before taking a final decision on an area where influencers have expertise knowledge.

EFFECT OF TRAVEL INFLUENCERS ON TOURISM INDUSTRY

Influencer marketing is an emerging tool in the field of marketing which got wider acceptance within a short span of time. Tourism industry is highly benefited from influencer marketing. Different researches on this area shows that influencer marketing has the power to bring changes in the behaviour of consumers. The pandemic covid-19 causes decline of tourists and decreases the traveling habits of people. But the emergence of various influencers helps to get back the tourism industry to somewhat in the normal stage. Travel influencers share all kinds of details regarding a destination which includes the facilities offered, safety, and further guidance etc. This makes more confidence in consumers who planned to travel. Social media provides such an extended platform in connecting with influencers and followers. Instagram is the highly recommended platform for influencer marketing.

CONCLUSION

With the emergence of globalization and digitization people, places, and products have started coming close, approachable as well as affordable. (Cetrez & Van Dam,2018). Introduction and development of internet technologies in India promotes the growth of online business and online marketing which in turn helps companies to market and sell their products and services through the online platform. Today every industry is conducting its activities through an online medium with an intension to increase their sales and gain more popularity among large number of consumers. Tourism industry requires innovative marketing techniques to attract more travelers. The role of travel influencers helps in the promotion of travel industry. Travel influencer can be considered as a new successful medium for marketing different products and services. The increased usage social media in the society creates more possible platforms for influencers and marketers.

REFERENCES

- Kshitij Mokhare, Atul Satpuli, Vaibhav Pal, Prajakta Badwaik (2021),'Impact of influencer marketing on travel and tourism', IJARIIE-ISSN (o)-2395-4396, v-7, issue-1, pg:1098-1105

- Appel, G., Grewal, L., Hadi, R., & Stephen, A. T. (2020). The future of social media in marketing. Mark. Sci. 48, 79–95. https://doi.org/10.1007/s11747-019-00695-1

- Asquith, J. (2019). Have Instagram influencers ruined travel for an entire generation?

- https://www.forbes.com.sites/jamesasquith/2019/09/01/have-instagram-influencers-ruined-travel-for-an-entiregeneration/#1f598621e30

- Cassia, F., & Magno, F. (2019). Assessing the Power of Social Media Influencers: A Comparison Between Tourism and Cultural Bloggers. Role of Consumer Trust. 10.24251/HICSS.2017.004.

- I Putu Gede Iwan Trisna Jaya, Ida Bagus Teddy Prianthara(2021),'Role of Social Media Influencers in Tourism Destination Image: How Does Digital Marketing Affect Purchase Intention?', DOI:10.2991/assehr.k.200331.114

- Rebekha Anna Pop, Zsuzsa Saplacan, Dan Cristian, Dabija and Monika Anetta Alt (2021), 'The impact of social media influencers on travel decisions: the role of trust in consumer decision journey', Current Issues in Tourism, DOI:10.1080/13683500.2 021.1895729

- Payal S Kapoor, M.S Balaji, Yang yang Jiang, Charles Jebarajakirthy (2021),' Effectiveness of Travel Social Media Influencers: A Case of Eco-Friendly Hotels', Journal of travel research, https://doi.org/10.1177/00472875211019469

- Linh Hale, Hancer, Murat (2021), 'Using social learning theory in examining you tube viewers desire to imitate travel vloggers', Journal of hospitality and tourism technology, DOI: 10.1108/JHTT-08-2020-0200

CHAPTER 15

SUSTAINABLE COASTAL TOURISM IN KERALA- ISSUES AND OPPORTUNITIES

Misha V,
Assistant Professor of Commerce,
Sree Narayana College, Kollam

ABSTRACT

While tourism is one of the world's most important sectors, coastal tourism is the fastest growing, with a significant increase in the last decade. Coastal tourism's economic significance is undeniable. For many governments and areas, it is one of the most important sources of revenue. Many coastal areas, which are particularly subject to pressures associated with its rise, have suffered significant socio-cultural, economic, physical, and environmental consequences as a result of this. Tourism benefits communities by creating jobs, increasing money through taxes, foreign exchange gains, and infrastructural development, among other things. It can promote cultural exchange between guests and hosts while also fostering greater understanding between people and cultures. By revitalizing traditional arts and crafts, sustainable tourism can also help to revitalize cultural and historical traditions. It can instil a sense of pride in local and national heritage, as well as a desire to preserve it. This article describes the issues and opportunities of sustainable coastal tourism in Kerala

Key Words: Coastal Tourism, Coastal environment, Coastal resource management,

INTRODUCTION

Kerala, named 'God's Own Country,' has risen to prominence as the country's most popular tourist destination. Kerala is a one-of-a-kind tourist destination due to its Ayurveda, beaches, backwaters, warm weather, hill stations, waterfalls, wild life, year-round festivals, and rich flora and fauna. As a significant source of money for the state's coffers, the state government has placed a strong priority on this industry. Tourists, the sites they visit, and the activities they participate in are all part of the tourism process. Coastal tourism, then, is tourism focused on the coastal area, including its natural and cultural features. It takes place along the shoreline and in the sea just off the shorelines.

Coastal environments are transitional zones between land and sea, with a high level of biodiversity. Mangroves and coral reefs, for example, are among the richest and most fragile ecosystems on the planet. At the same time, growing urbanization processes are putting a lot of pressure on the beaches. More than half of the world's population now lives near the sea (within 60 kilometres), and this number is growing. Furthermore, of all sections of the world, coastal areas are most visited by people, and tourism is the most important economic activity in many coastal towns. Scuba diving and snorkelling, wind surfing, fishing, observing marine mammals and birds, the cruise ship and ferry industries, all beach activities, sea kayaking, visits to fishing villages and lighthouses, maritime museums, sailing and motor yachting, maritime events, Arctic and Antarctic tourism, and many other activities are all included in coastal tourism.

Coastal tourism is one of the most popular types of travel. It is built on a unique resource combination at the land-sea interface that provides amenities like water, beaches, scenic beauty, rich terrestrial and marine biodiversity, diverse cultural and historic legacy, healthy cuisine, and, in most cases, strong infrastructure. It entails the development of tourism capacity (hotels, resorts, second homes, restaurants, and so on) as well as supporting infrastructure in both coastal zones and coastal seas (ports, marinas, fishing and diving shops, and other facilities).

Tourists and the people and places they visit, particularly the coastal environment and its natural and cultural riches, are all part of the coastal tourism process. The majority of coastal tourism occurs at the seashore and in the water immediately adjacent to it. Tourists now visit the seaside zone for portions of the day, weekends, short vacations, and extended stays. They may travel alone, with family, or in groups, depending on the circumstances. They may stay in a variety of coastal tourism accommodations, including tiny houses and camping sites that are rented out when chances occur, single bed-and-breakfast and hotel rooms, and luxury suites in resort enclaves.

With its fundamental qualities of sand, sea, and sun, coastal tourism is regarded one of the fastest developing areas of modern tourism. In order to build coastal ecosystems that are safe, stable, and appealing, with clean seas and healthy coastal habitats, the development of well-managed, long-term seaside tourism is essential. Aside from physical elements, the growth of tourism in coastal locations is influenced by socioeconomic factors such as local community interests, health and security conditions, political concerns such as unforeseen crises, and traditional tourism models. In recent decades, the expansion of tourism in coastal areas has reached a pinnacle.

The following are indicators of **Sustainable Coastal Tourism**:

➤ Coastal resource management and conservation plans are being developed. Program for industrial pollution control and environmental monitoring. Water, air, and healthy coastal eco-systems

➤ The management of coastal hazards such as erosion, storms, and floods ensures a safe and secure recreational environment.

➤ The Department of Forests, Environment, and Ecology has started mangrove rehabilitation and coastal plantation operations.

➤ We can appeal to a variety of groups within the coastal tourism segment, such as the young and adventurous who enjoy water sports, paragliding, and other activities, or travellers who want to experience the tranquilly, calm, and exclusivity.

➤ It is critical that each location's amenities and properties be developed. As a result, a parallel action to attract investors and developers to put up projects in these places must be undertaken, or we would see massive inflows into these areas with no capacity to handle these visitors, making the entire exercise a waste of time.

➤ Boaters, swimmers, and other water users should have acceptable levels of safety.

➤ Efforts to restore beaches' recreational and aesthetic values.

➤ Animal and habitat conservation policies that are sound.

➤ While efforts should be made to increase the number of tourists visiting coastal destinations, efforts should also be made to ensure that coastal ecosystems are protected so that there is no negative impact on the lives of local people as well as the health of our ocean and the creatures that live beneath it.

ISSUES OF COASTAL TOURISM

Coastal tourism is built on a unique resource combination at the land-sea interface: sun, water, beaches, breathtaking scenery, abundant biological diversity (birds, whales, corals, etc.), marine food, and well-developed transit infrastructure. Many coastal destinations in Kerala have established successful activities based on these advantages, such as well-maintained beaches, diving, boat rides, bird watching tours, restaurants, and medical facilities. Tourists today anticipate more than just sun, sea, and sand, as they did two decades ago. They are looking for a wide range of leisure activities and experiences, such as sports, cuisine, culture, and natural attractions. Locals in traditional tourist sites, on the other hand, are becoming increasingly concerned about protecting their own identity, the environment, and their natural, historic, and cultural assets from harmful consequences. The major issues of coastal tourism in Kerala are as follows:-

INFRASTRUCTURE FOR TOURISTS

Massive new tourist infrastructure has been constructed in several regions, including airports, marinas, resorts, and golf courses. Overdevelopment for tourism has the same issues as other coastal projects, but has a bigger impact because tourist developments are generally located close or at the edges of vulnerable marine habitats. Here are a few examples:

Mangrove forests and seagrass meadows have been cleared to make way for open beaches; tourist developments, such as piers and other structures, have been built directly on top of coral reefs; and endangered marine turtle nesting sites have been destroyed and disturbed by large crowds on the beaches.

FLOATING CITIES: CRUISE SHIPS

The popularity of cruise ships has had a negative impact on the maritime ecology. These massive floating ships, which carry on average 4,000 passengers and 1,670 staff, are a major cause of marine pollution due to the dumping of rubbish and untreated sewage at sea, as well as the release of other shipping-related pollutants.

ECOLOGICAL IMPACTS:

Tourism can put a lot of strain on local resources like energy, food, land, and water, which are already scarce. The direct local impacts of tourism on people and the environment at destinations are greatly affected by concentration in space and time. They are caused by the extensive use of water and land by tourist and leisure facilities, the delivery and use of energy, changes in the environment caused by the construction of infrastructure, structures, and services, and vegetation degradation and destruction.

RESORTS, OPERATORS, AND VISITORS WHO ARE IRRESPONSIBLE

The damage is caused by more than just tourism infrastructure construction. Some tourist resorts dump sewage and other trash into the sea near coral reefs and other vulnerable marine areas. Recreational activities have a significant impact as well. Careless boating, diving, snorkelling, and fishing, for example, have severely harmed coral reefs in many places of the world by causing people to touch reefs, stir up sediment, and drop anchors. Increased boat traffic and people approaching too closely harm marine wildlife such as whale sharks, seals, dugongs, dolphins, whales, and birds. Tourism can also increase seafood consumption in a region, putting strain on local fish populations and contributing to overfishing. The collection of corals, shells, and other marine souvenirs, whether by individual tourists or by locals who sell the souvenirs to tourists, has a negative impact.

EFFECTS ON BIODIVERSITY:

Tourism can reduce biodiversity in a variety of ways, such as by competing for habitat and natural resources with species. Specifically, a variety of causes can have a negative impact on biodiversity such as Socio-Cultural Consequences, Standardization and Local Culture Commercialization

OPPORTUNITIES OF COASTAL TOURISM

The fact of economic gains from seaside tourism has been established, and the most genuine thing is that the financial investment and profit is made by and for individuals who are not only physically but also socially far from the region. The global trend and reality is that tourism investors and developers put pressure on governments to spend public funds on infrastructure and services that are critical to the industry, as well as marketing campaigns that include tax cuts and other financial incentives (UNEP Division of Technology, Industry, and Economics, 2006). True, coastal tourism may result in more job opportunities, which can be beneficial economically, even attracting job seekers from beyond the local community. The major opportunities of Coastal tourism are as follows:-

CONTRIBUTION TO GOVERNMENT REVENUES

Government revenues from the coastal tourism sector in Kerala can be categorised as direct and indirect contributions. Direct contributions are generated by taxes from coastal tourism and employment due to tourism, tourism businesses and by direct charges on tourists.

FOREIGN EXCHANGE EARNINGS

Tourism expenditures, the export and import of related goods and services generate income to the host economy. Tourism is a main source of foreign exchange earnings for at least 38 % of all countries.

EMPLOYMENT GENERATION

The rapid expansion of international tourism has led to significant employment creation. Tourism can generate jobs directly through hotels, restaurants, taxis, souvenir sales and indirectly through the supply of goods and services needed by tourism-related businesses (e.g. conducted tour operators). Tourism represents around 7 % of the world's employees. Tourism can influence the local government to improve the infrastructure by creating better water and sewage systems, roads, electricity, telephone and public transport networks. All this can improve the standard of living for residents as well as facilitate tourism.

CONTRIBUTION TO LOCAL ECONOMIES

Tourism can be a significant or even an essential part of the local economy. As environment is a basic component of the tourism industry's assets, tourism revenues are often used to measure the economic value of protected areas. Part of the tourism income comes from informal employment, such as street vendors and informal guides. The positive side of informal or unreported employment is that the money is returned to the local economy and has a great multiplier effect as it is spent over and over again.

DIRECT FINANCIAL CONTRIBUTIONS TO NATURE PROTECTION

Tourism can contribute directly to the conservation of sensitive areas and habitats. Revenue from park-entrance fees and similar sources can be allocated specifically to pay for the protection and management of environmentally sensitive areas. Some governments collect money in more far-reaching and indirect ways that are not linked to specific parks or conservation areas. User fees, income taxes, taxes on sales or rental of recreation equipment and license fees for activities such as hunting and fishing can provide governments with the funds needed to manage natural resources.

COMPETITIVE ADVANTAGE

More and more tour operators take an active approach towards sustainability. Not only because consumers expect them to do so but also because they are aware are that intact destinations essential for the long term survival of the tourism industry. More and more tour operators prefer to work with suppliers who act in a sustainable manner, e.g. saving water and energy, respecting the local culture and supporting the wellbeing of local communities.

STRENGTHENING COMMUNITIES

Sustainable Coastal Tourism can add to the vitality of communities in many ways. For example through events and festivals of the local communities where they have been the primary participants and spectators. Often these are refreshed, reincarnated and developed in response to tourists' interests. The jobs created by tourism can act as a very important motivation to reduce emigration from rural areas. Local people can also increase their influence on tourism development, as well as improve their jobs and earnings prospects through tourism-related professional training and development of business and organizational skills.

ENCOURAGEMENT, SOCIAL INVOLVEMENT AND PRIDE

In some situations, tourism also helps to raise local awareness concerning the financial value of natural and cultural sites. It can stimulate a feeling of pride in local and national heritage and interest in its conservation. More broadly, the involvement of local communities in sustainable tourism development and operation seems to be an important condition for the sustainable use and conservation of the biodiversity.

CONCLUSION

Due to its major contribution to the economy, employment, revenue creation, and cultural promotion of the host country, tourism is one of the world's largest and fastest-growing economic industries. The tourism industry contributes 11% of the global GDP. It employs around 200 million people and carries nearly 700 million international passengers each year. By 2025, their numbers are predicted to double, posing a significant challenge for coastal environment. Coastal tourism is an evergreen tourist package among tourist subcategories. The natural beauty of seaside places has always attracted travelers. The natural beauty of each location should be preserved by appropriate policies implemented by the relevant authorities in order to reap the long-term benefits of tourism. In addition to the aforementioned conditions, some manmade improvements should be implemented on the beach in order to attract more youthful vacationers. The combination of natural beauty and man-made technologies for enjoying marine destinations can attract tourists from all over the world and improve the quality of Kerala's beaches.

REFERENCES

➤ Baitalik, A., & Majumdar, S.(2015). Coastal Tourism Destinations in West Bengal: Historical Background and Development. *International Journal of Social Sciences and Management*, 2(3), 267-272.

➤ Chandrashekhara, B., & Nagaraju, L.G. (2014). Coastal Tourism in Karnataka. *International Journal of Research in Humanities, Arts and Literature*, 6(2), 57-72.

➤ Noronha, L., Lourenço, N., Lobo Ferreira, J. P., Lleopart, A., Feoli, E., Sawkar, K., & Chachadi, A.(2002). Coastal tourism, environment, and sustainable development-a road map. *Tata Energy Research Institute*.

➤ Paul, A. K., Guha, S., & Kamila, A. (2017). Drivers of coastal tourism in Odisha state: a case study of Puri-Konark sites along the Bay of Bengal coast. *Journal of coastal sciences*, 1(4),6-19.

➤ https://www.keralatourism.org/destination/beaches/

➤ https://spb.kerala.gov.in/economic-review/ER2017/web_e/ch12.php?id=1&ch=12

CHAPTER 16

A STUDY ON THE FINANCIAL EFFECTS OF FLOOD ON THE PEOPLE OF THRISSUR DISTRICT

Andrea Varghese
Adhoc Faculty,
St Josephs College (Autonomous),
Irinjalakuda

Remya S.
Assistant Professor,
St Josephs College (Autonomous),
Irinjalakuda

ABSTRACT

This study deals with the analysis of financial effect of flood on people of Thrissur district. The information had been collected from the people using questionnaire.

The tools used are Percentage Analysis, Chi – Square Test, Weighted Average Mean and Z – Test. From this analysis it is clear that the flood had a bad effect on the financial aspects of the people and most of them responding negatively towards its after effects

INTRODUCTION

Flood has been considered as one of the most recurring and frequent disaster in the world. Due to recurrent prevalence, the economic loss and life damage caused by the flood has put more burdens on economy than any other natural disaster. It is already documented that climate change will lead to an intensification of the global water cycle with a consequent increase in flood hazard. Flood makes people vulnerable, as they take away their livelihoods at the first instance and leave them with little resources to overcome from the situation. Because of floods, rural poor communities face job loss, and two thirds of their income is reduced, which limits their capabilities of preparedness, responses, and recovery to subsequent floods. People cope with the situation by bearing substantial debts and loss of productive assets.

Kerala is in the aftermath of unfrequented flood havoc. The calamity has caused immeasurable misery and devastation. Hundreds of lives were lost. Thousands of homes were totally destroyed and many more were damaged, Keralites have braved the odds. Flooding problems induced by a changing climate would not be faced equally by all strata of society. Scholars claim that disasters have a disproportionate impact on the poor. It has been observed that the poor suffers the most and are more affected by any disaster that is, people who lack adequate means to take protective measures and those who have very little capacity to cope with the loss of property and income. Poverty is a significant contributor to people's vulnerability to flooding. Flood makes people vulnerable, as they take away their livelihoods at the first instance and leave them with little resources to overcome from the situation.

The impact of floods on the poor, especially those living in flood prone rural areas is even greater. The reasons behind this are lack of assets and inadequate food supplies. Flood not only deteriorates the social lives of the people but also the economy as a whole. It causes considerable damage to standing crops, livestock, poultry, houses, transportation and communication systems, educational and institutional buildings, and other social facilities. It also deteriorates the normal functions of life affecting homesteads, agricultural land, daily activities, water supply, sanitation condition and economic structure. These combined impacts on society, the economy and physical infrastructure jeopardize the livelihoods of the rural people. The poor are constantly struggling to cope with these impacts and manage their livelihoods.

Flood as one of the environmental hazards has possessed a serious danger risk to lives and properties of people in their environment. This project geared towards investigating the causes and effect of flood in Thrissur. The effect of flood has led to deplorable condition of living of people. Many people had either evacuated or abandoned their houses, farmlands were destroyed, commuters and transporters were faced with the problem of flooding in Thrissur area. Many parts of Kerala including Thrissur had been underwater for three days. Across Kerala, the total number of rain related deaths since May 29 rose to 357 on Sunday. For most of the residents in Thrissur district the disaster began to unfold on August 15 after days of incessant rain. When the gates of reservoirs were opened, rivers breached its banks. The strong currents washed away almost everything in their path. The damage that is caused to property, interruptions to the economy, and the impact on human health, also include the loss of life and injury, as well as outbreaks of diseases that can occur following the flood. An improved knowledge of flood impacts would enable the assessment of the vulnerability of cities and allow for the evaluation of different flood risk management strategies and their effectiveness.

Key words: Flood-Financial effect-Economic implication-Kerala Flood

2018 KERALA FLOODS

From 8th August 2018, severe floods affected the South Indian state of Kerala, due to unusually high rainfall during the monsoon season. It was the worst flood in Kerala in nearly a century. Over 483 people died, and 14 are missing. About a million people were evacuated, mainly from Chenganoor, Pandanad, Edanad, Aranmulla, Kozhanchery, Ayiroor, Ranni, Pandalam, Kuttanad, Malappuram, Aluva, Chalakudy, Thiruvalla, Eraviperoor, Valamkulam, N.Paravoor, Vypin Island and Palakkad. All fourteen districts of the state were placed on red alert. According to the Kerala Government, one sixth of the total population of Kerala had been directly affected by the floods and related incidents. The Indian government had declared it a level three calamity, or "calamity of a severe nature". It is the worst flood in Kerala after the great flood of 99 that took place in 1924.

THE ECONOMIC IMPLICATIONS OF THE KERALA FLOODS

Agriculture and Livestock

In terms of gross cropped area the three main crops in the state are coconut, rubber and paddy. Of these, the worst affected are paddy and rubber. One of the worst affected areas is Kuttanad – the rice bowl of the state. The area has been home to a number of poultry farmers, primarily duck hatcheries. The production areas of Idukki and Wayanad have been very adversely affected, as these are also the areas where landslips have been rampant. Loss of hoofed animals such as cows, goats, etc... are yet to be ascertained.

Service Sector and Tourism

The service sector accounts for about 63 percentage of Kerala's gross state value added and of which tourism alone accounts for about 10 percentage. The other two services that are complimentary to tourism are hotels, restaurants and retail trade, besides transportation. Some of the most important tourist spots are located in the districts of Idukki, Wayanad, Kottayam and Alappuzha. The recent floods have affected all the tourist spots, although efforts will be made to reopen them as quickly as possible.

The one saving grace is that Kerala is still open to business as Thiruvananthapuram and Kollam are not that much affected and tourist can still reach the state through the Thiruvananthapuram gateway. Also the tourism sector has shown great resilience and it is hoped to be back on its feet fairly soon. Even in the dark week of 13 August, there were no reports of tourists being holed up or trapped. If the rods can be repaired as quickly as possible, the sector can actually receive tourists from the forthcoming tourist season, which starts around October. The state will also have to deal with negative publicity that may be unleashed by other competing locals.

Consumer Goods

Kerala is considered as a large market for both consumer durables and non – durables alike. According to the recently released National Family Health Survey 2015-16, 30% of the households in Kerala have at least six of the following assets – house, electricity connection, mobile phone or a landline, air conditioner, refrigerator, TV, washing machine and motorized vehicle. People living in the worst affected areas may have lost or have to replace or repair some of these assets.

STATEMENT OF THE PROBLEM

The purpose of the study is to understand the effect of the flood over the people, especially focused on Thrissur district. The flood had an adverse effect on the people, especially on their house, farming and other properties. This study helps to gather information on monetary effect of flood on people and to analyze the perception of flood affected people. The primary research was carried out in order to find the data.

OBJECTIVES OF THE STUDY

1. To identify the major source depended on by the people for recovering

from the flood.

2. To assess the end result of the flood on various areas.

3. To examine whether the effect of flood on debt level is dependent on income level.

SIGNIFICANCE OF THE STUDY

The significance of this project is laid on to understand the actual value and real depth of the losses that occurred in Thrissur district due to flood. This study also helps to understand the period taken to recover from the flood.

SCOPE OF THE STUDY

The scope of the study is wider and hence it is limited to selected respondents of different Panchayath in Thrissur district who had been affected by flood during August 2018. The study focuses only on the financial effects caused by flood.

RESEARCH METHODOLOGY

Research Design

Analytical and descriptive research designs are used for the study.

Population of the Study

The study is conducted among flood affected people in Thrissur district.

Sample Unit

The Sample Unit is various Municipalities and Panchayath of Thrissur district.

Sample Size

From the population, 50 samples have taken for the research study.

Sampling Technique

Convenience sampling is used for the study.

Data Collection

The study was mainly based on primary data. This study is both analytical and descriptive. The primary data has been collected through administering questionnaire. Personal interview with the flood affected people has been adopted for the purpose of obtaining first hand information. Various journals and websites were also used for reference.

Tools used for Analysis

- ➤ Percentage Analysis
- ➤ Weighted Average Mean
- ➤ Z- test
- ➤ Chi – Square test

Hypothesis for the Study

- ➤ Effect of flood is equal on various factors.
- ➤ The two attributes, income level and affect on debt level are independent.

LITERATURE REVIEW

Panos Varagis, Jerry Seeks and Paul Siegel (2002)[1] in their study "Can Financial Markets be Trapped to Help Poor People to Cope with Weather Risks?" have remarked that, poor households in rural areas are particularly vulnerable to risks that reduce incomes and increase expenditures. Most past research has focused on risk coping strategies for the rural poor, specifically on micro-level and household actions. These are risks that can be shared within a community or extended family. These strategies are effective for independent risks, but ineffective for covariate or systematic risks. **Bimal Kanti Paul (2003)**[2] in his study " Relief Assistance to 1998 Flood Victims: a Comparison of the Performance of the Government and NGOs" stated that, with increasing support from the international community, non-governmental organizations (NGOs) have played an important role in Bangladesh since the early 1970s in providing emergency assistance to disaster victims. Respondent opinions regarding emergency relief distribution suggest that both sources performed satisfactorily and an overwhelming majority of them thought that the government performed better than it had previously in distributing relief assistance to flood victims. Following an analysis of the survey data, this paper discusses the policy implications for future disaster assistance efforts in Bangladesh and elsewhere **Emmanuel Skoufias (2003)**[3] in his paper "Economic Crises and Natural Disasters: Coping Strategies and Policy Implications" reviews 12 studies presented at a conference examining two broad themes: 1) the interplay between household coping strategies and the impact of crises and natural disasters on various dimensions of well being(example: consumption and child nutrition); and 2) some of the ex-ante and ex-post strategies that public agencies can adopt so they can be more effective in protecting households and their members from the potentially adverse impacts of aggregate shocks. **Michael K Lindell and Carla S Peter (2003)**[4] in their study, "Assessing Community Impacts of Natural Disasters" have opined that, community impacts of natural disasters has yielded a wide variety of findings, but no coherent model of the process by which hazard agent characteristics produce physical and social impacts. This article summarizes the principal features of this process and describes the way in which hazard mitigation and emergency preparedness practices can limit the physical impacts and the way in which community recovery resources and extra community assistance can reduce social impacts.**Charlotte Benson and Edward Clay (2004)**[5] in their report "Understanding the Economic and Financial Impacts of Natural Disasters" have remarked that, the macro-economic and public finance implications of natural disasters, including the role of information and mechanisms for risk spreading, and drawing in particular on evidence from Bangladesh, Dominica and Malawi. Major natural disasters can have severe negative short-run economic and budgetary impacts. Disasters also appear to have adverse longer-term consequences for economic growth, development and poverty reduction

DATA ANALYSIS AND INTERPRETATION

Chi – Square test is a statistical test, which tests the significance of difference between observed frequencies and the corresponding theoretical frequencies of a distribution, without any assumptions about the distribution of the population. To test whether the two attributes, income level and effect on debt level are independent or not Chi – Square test is used.

H_0. The two attributes, income level and effect on debt level are independent.

Table 1: Observed Values

Debt level Income Level	Not Increased	Increased	Total
<10,000	5	23	28
>10,000	7	15	22
Total	12	38	50

(Source: Primary Data)

$$X^2 = \frac{(ad - bc)^2\, N}{(a+b)\,(c+d)\,(a+c)\,(b+d)}$$

$$= 1.317$$

Degree of freedom $= (r - 1)\,(c - 1) = 1$

Table value $= 3.8415$

As the calculated value is less than table value, we accept the null hypothesis that is; two attributes income level and debt level are independent. So, the flood had increased the debt level of the respondents irrespective of income level.

From the above table, it is clear that flood had increased the debt level and it is not dependent on their income level. So, it is evident that flood had a greater effect on rich and poor equally and it also raised their debt level as the financial assistance from the government was not adequate to meet the after effects of flood.

WEIGHTED AVERAGE MEAN

Weighted Average Mean is a mean calculated by giving values in a data set according to some attributes of the data. In order to analyze the other sources relied on by the people to recover from the flood if the financial assistance from the government is not adequate.

Table 2: Other Sources Relied to Recover from Flood

Sl. No.	Particulars	Weight	6	5	4	3	2	1	Total	Mean Score	Rank
1	Kudumbashree Loan	F	13	11	4	1	4	1	34	4.74	I
		Fx	78	55	16	3	8	1	161		
2	Donations from Private Parties	F	3	8	8	7	6	2	34	3.68	IV
		Fx	18	40	32	21	12	2	125		
3	Bank Loan	F	5	7	12	3	3	4	34	3.88	III
		Fx	30	35	48	9	6	4	132		
4	Loan from Private Parties/ Institutions	F	6	6	7	12	3	0	34	4	II
		Fx	36	30	28	36	6	0	136		
5	Panchayath	F	3	0	3	9	14	5	34	2.65	V
		Fx	18	0	12	27		5	90		
6	Others	F	4	2	0	2	4		34	2.06	VI
		Fx	24	10	0	6	8		70		

(Source: Primary Data)

From the above table it is clear that, among the six sources Kudumbashree Loans are depended more and next is Loan from Private Parties/ Institutions, third comes the Bank Loan, fourth is Donations from Private Parties, fifth is Panchayath and Other sources are least depended.

SCALING TECHNIQUE

Scaling Technique is used to measure variable related with effect of flood on a three point scale with a weightage of three, two, one for no effect, moderate effect and severe effect.

Table 3: Effect of Flood on Various Factors

Sl. No.	Factors	Effect of Flood											
		No Effect			Moderate Effect			Severe Effect			Total		
		R	%	S	R	%	S	R	%	S	R	%	S

1	Agricultural Production	15	30	45	16	32	32	19	38	19	50	100	96
2	Livestock	19	38	57	19	38	38	12	24	12	50	100	107
3	Health	21	42	63	19	38	38	10	20	10	50	100	111
4	Housing	1	2	3	25	50	50	24	48	24	50	100	77
5	Other Properties	3	6	9	20	40	40	27	54	27	50	100	76

(Source: Primary Data)

R: Respondents, %: Percentage, S: Score

From the above table it is clear that, 98 percentage of respondents claimed that flood has effected on housing, 94 percentage opined that it affected other properties, 70 percentage on agricultural production, 62 percentage on livestock and 58 percentage on health.

Z – TEST

Z – Test is a statistical test applied when the test statistic follows normal distribution. It is used to test the given population mean when the sample is large or when the population standard deviation is known. Here it is used to test whether the difference between effect on individual factors and effect of flood is same or not.

Hypothesis for the test

Effect of flood is equal on various factors

Sub – Hypothesis

1. There is no significant difference between effect on Agricultural Production and overall effect of flood.

2. There is no significant difference between effect on Livestock and overall effect of flood.

3. There is no significant difference between effect on Health and overall effect of flood.

4. There is no significant difference between effect on Housing and overall effect of flood.

5. There is no significant difference between effect on Other Properties and overall effect of flood.

Table 4: Z Value of Factors

Sl. No.	Factors	Mean	Standard Deviation	Standard Error	Z Value
1	Agricultural Production	1.92	0.829	0.1172	0.444
2	Livestock	2.14	0.783	0.1107	2.457
3	Health	2.22	0.764	0.1080	3.259
4	Housing	1.54	0.542	0.0767	4.276
5	Other Properties	1.52	0.614	0.0868	4.009
6	Grand Mean	1.868			

Critical value of Z at 5 percentage level of significance is 1.96

Sub – Hypothesis 2,3,4,5 are rejected. So there is significant difference between effect on Livestock, Health, Housing, Other Properties and overall effect of flood. And main hypothesis is rejected since the effect of flood is not equal among various factors.

From the above table it can be concluded that, overall effect of flood is 1.868. This indicates that flood has effected on most of the factors in moderate or severe manner. The effect on Livestock and Health is considerably greater than this value that is 2.14 and 2.22. But effect on Housing and Other Properties is considerably lower than this value that is 1.54 and 1.52. From the Z-Test it is clear that flood least affected the Livestock and Health and most affected the Housing and Other Properties when compared to other factors. Effect of flood on Agricultural Production is almost equal to the overall effect of flood.

OTHER FINDINGS

1. More than 50 percentage of the respondents are having an average income of approximately less than Rs.10,000.

2. 80 percentage of the respondents are not affected by any waterborne diseases and 50 percentage of the affected people had incurred more than Rs.500 rupees to cure the disease.

3. Loss of belongings had found a major problem for 92 percentage

of the respondents and 57 percentage of them incurred more than Rs.40,000 as replacement cost of belongings.

4.   70 percentage of the respondents did not have any insurance for their property. So, they are facing more financial effect after the flood.

5.   Among the respondents who are having insurance for their property, 80 percentage of them are paying more than Rs.300 as monthly insurance premium.

6.   70 percentage of the respondents did not have any valid insurance claim.

7.   90 percentage of respondents had received financial assistance from the government. But, for 64 percentage of them the fund was not adequate to meet the after effects of flood.

8.   Flood had increased the debt level of 76 percentage of the respondents and it is moderately or highly increased for 74 percentage of them.

9.   Among the respondents, 62 percentage found to had a greater effect of flood on their remuneration.

10. 64 percentage of respondents had taken more than a month to recover from the after effects of flood.

11. The effect of flood on the debt level of the respondent is irrespective of their income level.

12.   Respondents are depending on loans from Kudumbashree and Private Parties/ Institutions the most to recover from the flood. Least depended on Other Sources.

13. Flood had a greater effect on Other Properties and Housing. Least effect on Livestock and Health.

SUGGESTIONS

1.   Government should take adequate steps to provide more monetary assistance for the flood effected people.

2.   Government should take necessary steps to replace the damaged housing properties and belongings during flood.

3.   Measures may be taken to ensure that the flood affected families receive financial assistance from their own Panchayath.

4. People should try to take insurance policies for their properties especially for house, vehicles and other properties to reduce the burden of loss during the natural calamities in future.

5. Banks and other institution should expand the time limit for the repayment of loans to the flood affected people.

CONCLUSION

The study titled **"A Study on the Financial Effects of Flood on the People of Thrissur District"** aims to discover how flood affected the families of Thrissur district. And the study revealed that the flood created an outflow of money from the families. Majority had to spend at least 50,000 rupees to replace their lost belongings. Even if everyone had received financial assistance from the government, it was not enough to recover from the flood. So, the debt level of majority has increased and mostly they depended on Other Sources and Panchayath. And flood had seriously affected housing and other properties.

It can be concluded that flood had a greater financial effect of people who had faced this vulnerability. And effect of flood on various factors is not uniform. But we can hope that the present difficulties can be solved by availing more assistance from the Government in monetary terms. And people should be ready to face such calamities in the future.

REFERENCES

> Panos Varangis, Jerry Seeks, Paul Seigel, "Can Financial Markets be Trapped to Help poor People to Cope with Whether Risks?", *The World Bank Report,*2002.

> Bimal Kanti Paul, "Relief Assistance to 1998 Flood Victims: a Comparison between Government and NGOs", *The Geographical Journal*, Vol.169,

> Issue -1, May 2003, pp 18 – 30.

> Emmanuel Skoufias, "Economic crises and Natural Disasters: Coping Strategies and Policy Implications", *World Development*, Vol.31, Issue-7, November 2003, pp 1087 – 1102.

> Michael K Lindell, Carla S Prater, " Assesing Community Impacts of Natural Disasters" , *Natural Hazards Review*, Vol. 4, Issue- 4, November 2003,

> pp 176-185.

> Charlotte Benson, Edward Clay, "Understanding the Economic and Financial Impacts of Natural Disasters", *The World Bank Report*, 2004.

CHAPTER 17

ROLE OF TOURISM SECTOR IN INDIAN ECONOMY: A REVIEW

Dr. Dinesh Kumar Gupta
Assistant Professor, Department of Economics
Government Degree College Banbasa (Champawat)
{Affiliated to Soban Singh Jeena University, Almora (Uttarakhand)}

ABSTRACT

Today India is known for various categories of tourism, such as adventure tourism, medical tourism, eco-tourism, rural tourism, etc. The growing influence of the tourism sector as an economic powerhouse and its potential as a tool for development of Indian economy. Tourism sector not only spearhead the growth; it also improves the people's lives standard with its capacity to create large scale employment of diverse kind. It supports environmental protection, diverse cultural heritage and strengthens peace in the world. The challenges faced by this sector can be overcome. Surely the Indian tourism sector has grown at a rapid pace in the last few years.

Keywords: Tourism, Economic Growth, Balance of Payment, Foreign Exchange, Employment.

INTRODUCTION

Tourism industry occupies a unique place in India as it is one of the major emerging segments of our economy. It attracts and also brings huge foreign currency and generates employment in our economy. In the era of globalisation, the travel and tourism activities have increased significantly. United Nation's World Tourism Organisation has forecasted that international tourism would continue to grow at an average annual rate of 4%. In current time tourism has become the largest and profitable industry in the world. In this circumstances, the natural, cultural and historical heritage of India makes it a very important from the point of view of tourism. Today India is known for various categories of tourism, such as adventure tourism, medical tourism, eco-tourism, rural tourism, etc. It is also known that in India from Kashmir to Kanyakumari and from Arunachal Pradesh to Gujarat, each region has its own uniqueness and culture. These regions have the potential to attract tourists with their natural features such as cold/hot deserts, rivers, forests (Niligiri and North East), Islands (Andaman and Nicobar), mountains and plateaus. Also, the wide variety of landscapes and cultural heritage found here are providing many options for tourists coming from abroad. Even today in some countries of the world (such as Sri Lanka, Nepal, Bhutan, Myanmar etc.) where followers of Hinduism, Buddhism and Jainism live in large numbers. It is worth mentioning that due to the birthplace of the originator of these religions, there are a large number of holy and religious tourist places, due to which tourists from Southeast and East Asian countries are attracting in large numbers.

EMERGING DIMENSIONS IN TOURISM

Apart from traditional tourism, new type of tourism activities is being created.

1. Health tourism

2. Spiritual tourism

3. Adventure tourism

4. Meetings, Incentives, Conferences and Exhibitions (MICE) tourism

5. Rural tourism

6. Sustainable tourism

India has been got third rank of the World Travel and Tourism Council (WTTC) report, 2018. The report looked at the performance of 185 countries over the past seven years (2011-2017). There were seen four main pillars of this report-

1. Total Contribution into GDP

2. International travel expenses

3. Domestic tourism expenses and

4. Capital investment

This can be called a huge achievement for India in terms of raising its position at these four levels. In the year 2017, India generated around $23 billion in revenue from tourism, which is targeted to reach $100 billion by 2023. This is higher than in France and Spain. It is noteworthy that in 2017 India had 14 million foreign tourists, whereas in 2014 the same figure was 768 lakh. In this context, India has registered an annual growth of 14% on the tourism front, which is much higher than the global average of 6.8% and the Asian average of 5.7%. However, the growth of domestic tourism was only 2.3%. The contribution of tourism to the GDP is 7%.

REVIEW OF LITERATURE

Tourism sector is one of the fastest development service industry with huge possibilities future in the world. Due to growth of this sector more economic profit of the country such as growth of income, employment and taxes. (Archer,1995; Balaguer and Cantavella Jorda,2002). Tourism sector provide more assets to the countries such as foreign exchange which are more needful to import of capital goods and technology for economic growth. (Kim et, 2006; Arslanturk et al, 2011). Tourism sector is also providing job opportunities for skilled and unskilled labour. The development of this sector boosts the whole economy which generates huge foreign currency earnings, also boosts revenue and encourages income and live standard of the people (Rani & Gupta, 2016). Development of tourism sector has given to job creation, foreign exchange, infrastructure, investment, economic growth etc. Due to tourism sector growth, India has able to sustained and inclusive growth (Dayananda.K.C. & D.S. Leelavathi, 2016). Tourism sector is the main source of job creation and raising the foreign exchange for the island countries and dominant economic sector (Ghose,2011)

OBJECTIVE OF THE STUDY

➤ To find the contribution of this sector in growth of Indian economy.

➤ To describes the opportunities in tourism sector

➤ To find the challenges of this sector

RESEARCH METHODOLOGY

This research paper describes about tourism and its impact on Indian economy. For the study of the object of this paper we have to used secondary data and sources for finding result. In the secondary sources we have taken support of the magazine, different research paper, newspaper, government sites and various report of tourism sector.

RESULT & DISCUSSION

Role of tourism sector in Indian Economy:

The growing influence of the tourism sector as an economic powerhouse and its potential as a tool for development of Indian economy. Tourism sector not only spearhead the growth; it also improves the people's lives standard with its capacity to create large scale employment of diverse kind. It supports environmental protection, diverse cultural heritage and strengthens peace in the world.

The key figures relating to financial performance of the Corporation for the last Five years (In Cr. Rs.) are tabulated below:

Table-1

Items	2015-16	2016-17	2017-18	2018-19	2019-20
Turnover	465.69	356.11	366.42	371.72	357.49
Profit before Tax	32.42	17.00	21.25	57.91	37.57
Profit after tax	22.5	11.43	17.71	42.15	22.48
Foreign Exchange Earnings	17.95	15.20	15.27	18.65	16.11

Source: Annual Report 2020-21 Ministry of Tourism Government of India

Contribution of tourism to GDP and employment:

Table - 2

Items	2013-14	2014-15	2015-16	2016-17	2017-18	2018-19
Share in GDP (In %)	5.68	5.81	5.09	5.04	5.00	5.00
Share in Jobs (In %)	11.91	12.14	12.38	12.2	12.29	12.95
Direct & Indirect Jobs due to tourism (In Million)	67.19	69.56	72.26	75.71	80.54	88.72

Source: Annual Report 2020-21 Ministry of Tourism Government of India

In the Indian economy the total transactions of tourism sector are increasing continuously from 2014 to 2019. Rate of the profit, Employment opportunities and foreign exchange earning in this sector are also increasing. We found from the table-2 that contribution of this sector into GDP has increased.

TOP 10 SOURCE COUNTRIES FOR FOREIGN TOURIST ARRIVALS (FTAS) IN INDIA IN 2020

Table-3

S.N.	Source Country	Percentage Share
1	Bangladesh	20.01
2	United States	14.36
3	United Kingdom	10.63
4	Canada	4.48
5	Russian Federation	3.72
6	Australia	3.16
7	France	2.70
8	Germany	2.64
9	Malaysia	2.55
10	Sri Lanka	2.50
	Total	66.76
	Others	32.94
	Grand Total	100.00

Source: Bureau of Immigration, Govt. of India (2020)

PROSPECTS OF TOURISM SECTOR:

Tourism sector in India contributed a positive impact on the Balance of Payment from which it plays an important role regarding increasing foreign exchange earnings in India. The annual growth rate of this Industry in India is 9.4%. This Industry will support for about 46 million jobs by 2025. International Tourist's arrival in India is expected to reach 30.5 billion by 2028. Various projects under the Swadesh Darshan and Prasad scheme has been sanctioned of worth Rs 550 crore (US$ 78.70 million).

Challenges in Tourism Sector: There are some major challenges in the field of tourism sector, which are given below.

➤   A slow process for Visa facility is more creating issues in this sector.

➤ Low awareness: Low awareness of the e-visa facility in this sector makes the entry process quite difficult for tourists.

➤ Limited entry on e-Visa is challenging in this sector.

➤ Deficiencies in infrastructure like sanitation, living facilities, hotels, etc., and inadequate connectivity hamper tourist visits to heritage sites.

➤ Low level of skilled of individuals for the tourism sector is a major challenge for providing visitors a world-class experience.

➤ Slow and low of marketing policy is a main concern for tourist places. Also, the campaigns of tourism sector are poorly managed. All these issues affect the tourism industry of the region.

➤ Sanitation and health system- Lack of sanitation in major cities have caused a negative impact on Indian food and public health care.

➤ Few areas of Indian economy still poor electricity. Even access to information to domestic and foreign tourists is not at ease.

➤ Tourism has also caused environmental concerns in the hills and the beaches.

CONCLUSION:

The challenges faced by this sector can be overcome. Surely the Indian tourism sector has grown at a rapid pace in the last few years. Due to the promotion of this sector, the country's GDP, foreign exchange earnings and the number & percentage of employment have also increase. Indian economy has the potential to boost tourism along with natural beauty. Development of tourism sector enhances the capacity of other sectors such as infrastructure, transport, communication, hotel etc. After analysis of the economic effects of this sector we found that tourism services have extremely beneficial effects on employment and the current balance of payments in the Indian economy.

REFERENCE

➤ Annual Report 2020-21 Ministry of Tourism Government of India

➤ Archer, B., (1995), "Importance of tourism for the economy of Bermuda", Annals of Tourism Research, 22 (4), 918–930.

➤ Bureau of Immigration, Govt. of India (2020)

- Dayananda.K.C, & D.S.Leelavathi. (2016). Tourism Development and Economic Growth in India. Journal of Humanities And Social Science, 21(11). doi:10.9790/0837-2111084349

- E- Book of Ministry of Tourism 2017-18

- Ghosh, T. (2011). Coastal Tourism: Opportunity and Sustainability. Journal of Sustainable Development, 4(6), 67-71

- https://ambassade-ethiopie.fr/onewebmedia/Tourism-WTTC-Global-Economic-Impact-Trends-2019.pdf

- https://tourism.gov.in/flipbook/1

- https://www.jatinverma.org/tourism-in-india-opportunities-and-challenges-air.

- India Tourism Statistics at a Glance- 2021, Ministry of Tourism Government of India.

- Kim, H.J., Chen, M.H., Jang, S.C., (2006), "Tourism expansion and economic development: The case of Taiwan", Tourism Management, 27(5), 925–933.

- World Travel and Tourism Council (WTTC) report, 2018

CHAPTER 18

FARM TOURISM-AN EMERGING TOURIST DESTINATION

Anu Varghese
Assistant.Professor,
St. John's College, Anchal, University of Kerala

INTRODUCTION

Tourism in India is a fast-growing business. Tourism is becoming a more essential and diverse part of local development, particularly in terms of reviving and reorganizing local economies and boosting quality of life. Tourist flows can provide at least supplemental revenue in the agricultural, artisan, and service sectors. India is a country that is surrounded by the Indian Ocean, Himalayas, Bay of Bengal, and Arabian Sea, and has several unique places that are notable for their cultural heritage, historic importance, diverse climatic conditions, wildlife reserves, natural beauty and so on. Tourists can partake in a variety of activities such as ecotourism, health tourism, adventure tourism, cultural tourism, heritage tourism, wildlife tourism, religious tourism, farm tourism, rural tourism and so on. Only in India, can travellers enjoy all of these types of tourism at the same time. Tourism is frequently accused of having a negative impact on our environment, natural resources, and other factors.

Encouraging 'Farm Tourism' is a novel approach to this problem. In addition to boosting tourism, 'Farm Tourism' contributes to the preservation of the natural balance by emphasizing the importance of natural resources. Farm tourism is one of the five categories of rural tourism and is one of the fastest expanding areas in tourism. Kerala, as an agriculturally oriented society, has a plethora of opportunities to create farm tourism. Tourists that come to Kerala often want to see the lush greenery. If given the opportunity to explore nature, they will take advantage of it. Promotion of so-called "farm tourism" does not necessitate a significant increase in investment. The World Tourism Organization defined the principles of sustainable tourism in 1988 as "leading to the management of all resources in such a way that economic, social, and aesthetic needs can be met while maintaining cultural integrity, essential ecological processes, biological diversity, and life support systems." Due to widespread concern about the social and environmental implications of mass tourism, ecotourism and farm tourism have grown in popularity since the 1980s. Farm tourism is one of the greatest sustainable tourist techniques because the size of development is better linked to local resources and institutional capabilities.

LITERATURE REVIEW

(Barbieri et al., 2019).Farm tourism is viewed as a viable financial option for farmers who are experiencing lower profits and problems as a result of the agricultural crisis and restructuring. Educational utility, cross-marketing utility, and enhancing agritourism epistemology are some of the unmeasured potential benefits of agritourism.

Sonnino (2004) Agritourism as hospitality-related activities carried out by agricultural entrepreneurs and their families, where these activities are linked to and complementary to farming activities.

 (Lupi et al., 2017) For farmers, the pursuit of self-values and revenue growth are the most essential elements in deciding whether or not to participate in agritourism. Agritourism also helps to ensure agricultural sustainability, which is becoming increasingly important beyond national borders.

STATEMENT OF THE PROBLEM

Agriculture is one of the most important contributors to the Indian economy; around 52 percent of the population is directly or indirectly dependent on agriculture, According to the Economic Survey 2020-2021, agriculture's contribution of GDP has risen to nearly 20% for the first time in 17 years, making it the only bright light in GDP performance in 2020-21. The phrase 'farm tourism' first appeared in international literature in the last quarter of the twentieth century. Farm tourism is growing increasingly popular nowadays. Kerala is a state where a variety of agricultural crops are grown. In this case, the paper aims to study the gaining prominence of Farm Tourism.

OBJECTIVES OF THE STUDY

1. To understand the concept of Farm tourism

2. To study the significance of Farm tourism in Kerala

3. To suggest the measures for the prospects of Farm tourism

METHODOLOGY

This study is descriptive in nature purely based on secondary information collected from the various government official websites, journals, books, research articles and reports from Newspapers and Magazines.

FARM TOURISM

Agriculture is the backbone of the Indian economy, and farm tourism is one of the most recent innovations in the Indian tourism business. Tourism as a business began in places with natural or man-made attractions that drew visitors for a variety of leisure activities in a variety of settings. Later, tourism took on other forms, with Farm-tourism being one of the most recent to emerge. Farm-tourism, according to the World Tourism Organization, is "offering lodging at the farmhouse, providing meals, and organizing and aiding tourists' participation in various farming operations."During the visit, travellers will be able to experience a really magical and authentic contact with rural life, original local cuisine, and learn about various farming jobs.

The tourist industry has recently experienced steady expansion and has gained global prominence as a key industry. It has economic, social, cultural, and environmental ramifications that reach practically every corner of the globe. However, the tourism industry is at a fork in the road, and it is trying to cope with the resulting environmental consequences. Many industry actors, notably those in the ecotourism sector, which is the subject of this special section, do not fully define environmental and social responsibilities.

Farm lodging, local food and beverage, festivals, nature observation, you-pick (harvest) activities, educational and recreational trips, hunting, fishing, and gift sales are all examples of agri-tourism activities and services. It was seen as a low-risk, low-investment strategy in many areas because farms primarily used their existing resources. It's the temporary relocation of persons seeking to enjoy a rural setting as part of their leisure, enjoyment, recreation, or business activities to a farm. The key reason for moving forward with this is because The idea is that it can help with overall income, cash flow, and profitability.Farm-based business profitability It will provide the farmer another option. source of income from the farm's output and can involve farm members.

Farm tourism, which is an important component of eco-tourism, has proven to be a highly effective tourism initiative in Kerala. It protects the farmers' agricultural interests while also providing them with additional money from tourist visits to the property. Farmers may now sell their products to a new set of buyers: tourists.In most farms that include tourism activities, organic farming and allied development approaches are used. These farms do not have any artificial gardens or ponds, and no pesticides are employed.Tourists can tour farms and learn about farming techniques. The trip to such a farm is enjoyable in and of itself.

EVOLUTION OF FARM TOURISM

The phrase 'Farm-tourism' was coined in the United States, but it was first used in Italy in 1985 as part of a National Legal Framework. This statute encourages overnight farm stays in order to diversify Italian farmers' incomes and preserve the landscape of farming operations. The foundation of the Agri Tourism Development Corporation (ATDC) in Baramati, Maharashtra, sowed the seeds of farm tourism in India. Pandurang Taware, an entrepreneur from the rural community, launched the ATDC in 2004.

It is a Maharashtra-based organization that promotes farm tourism as a means of expanding business prospects and ensuring a sustainable livelihood for farmers. The ATDC has evolved, with some educated farmers and agri-tourism venues around Maharashtra, following a phase of study and an initial pilot programme in a village of Baramati district in 2005. Farmers in the state have seen a 25% increase in their revenue since the programme began.

The Indian government has set a goal of doubling farmers' incomes by 2022. However, economic data reveal that this is not a case of equitable and egalitarian growth. Farm-tourism can be introduced as a supplementary sector to augment and boost farmers' incomes. However, in India, policies and norms for this notion are still lacking.

PROSPECTS AND PROBLEMS OF FARM TOURISM

Policies and subsidies aimed specifically towards farm tourism are critical. To improve agri-tourism income, regional development plans and models are also required for the effective use of local resources and the establishment of vital services for tourists in a specific region.

As a result, farmers can convert their farmlands into tourism attractions and open their doors to the public to offer more information about what they do. Simultaneously, they can increase their revenue while simultaneously increasing the value of their farm produce.

Kerala has an agrarian economy, with a network of blue backwaters, rivers, and streams. The state's principal agricultural products are rice, coconut, tapioca, spices, tea, coffee, cashew, lentils, areca nut, ginger, and rubber. Farm tourism is a relatively new tourism product being promoted in Kerala. Kerala, as a predominantly agricultural state, has enormous potential to grow farm tourism in a large way without a lot of additional expenditure. Despite having unique and different agro-climatic conditions in several places that allow it to cultivate a wide range of crops, the state's agricultural legacy is not on par with that of other states. With minimal involvement, it is possible to convert prospective agricultural regions of the state into tourist destinations, allowing the advantages of tourism to flow directly to the farmers.Farm tourism is a relatively new kind of tourism. Kerala offers numerous chances for agriculture tourism. There is no need to create anything here. They occur naturally, and they can be promoted naturally. Farm and plantation tourism can be found in the locations like Idukki,Wayanadu,Palakkad,Kuttanadu,Pathanamthitta,Kottayam:Farmers today provide a variety of services to entice visitors to the agricultural area. Farm tourism includes the following activities:-

➤ Choosing to stay on a farm

➤ Sports in the open air

➤ Participation in rural lifestyles and communities

➤ enjoyment of the natural world

➤ Cultural activities during the processing and production tour

➤ Hut type restaurants serving a variety of cuisines

➤ House in the tree

> Boating, hunting, fishing, and hiking are some of the activities available.

It is difficult to make the shift from traditional agriculture to farm-tourism. One important challenge is developing products and services that tourists want. Increased disposable income combined with shorter working days leads to increased demand for leisure activities, which helps farm-tourism thrive.

GOVERNMENT INITIATIVES FOR FARM TOURISM

The tourist department plans to implement a host of creative programmes stressing farm tourism and homestead farming as part of its efforts to resuscitate the state's Covid-ravaged tourism sector.The Kerala state government intends to create micro destination spots around the state, with at least one tourism station in each local government. Steps are being taken in this direction, and the government has already begun training for LSGD representatives. Tourism activities will be included in the general subjects of local self-government bodies, and some of their projects will be related to the tourism industry. The tourism department has also taken steps to implement a bio-bubble system in the business by vaccination all players. While Vythiri in Wayanad has become the state's first 100 percent vaccinated tourism destination, vaccination is also progressing in other areas.

In two years, the objective of Government is to build 500 farm tourism units and 5,000 homestead agricultural areas around the state and link them to tourism activities, in order to improve the tourism department's 'village life experience' programme. The job of integrating farming into village life activities in tourism programmes has been allocated to the Responsible Tourism (RT) Mission.

SUGGESTIONS

> Education and counseling for stakeholders participating in farm tourism must be provided.

> Participation of women's self-help groups in conservation programs will aid in the growth of farm tourism.

> More nature friendly facilities should be built using environmentally friendly techniques such as solar energy, rainwater capture and reuse, garbage recycling, natural cross-ventilation instead of air

conditioning, and high-level self-sufficiency in food production through ecological farms and aquaculture, among others.

- ➤ To encourage the use of natural on-farm inputs for chemical-free farming, the Bharatiya Prakritik Krishi Padhati (BPKP) of PKVY has to launch more campaigns for farmers to promote natural farming.

- ➤ Community based Facebook groups should post and promote farmtourism events in various facebook groups for gaining mass attention.

- ➤ NSS,Scouts and various clubs functioning in schools and Colleges can collaborate with panchayaths and ministries for promoting farm events.

CONCLUSION

Tourism in natural places should be environmentally friendly. A visitor should be able to participate in the learning process. It can be used to promote environmental protection, local empowerment, and poverty alleviation, among other things. As a result, it necessitates careful planning based on regulations. Farm tourism will continue to flourish as a viable way of life in numerous regions of the world in the future, and how sustainable it will be in the future under the entrance of tourists from other nations is unknown.

REFERENCES

- ➤ Barbieri, C. (2019). Agritourism research: A perspective article.Tourism Review,75(1), 149–152

- ➤ Lupi, C., Giaccio, V., Mastronardi, L., Giannelli, A., & Scardera, A.(2017). Exploring the features of agritourism and its contribution to rural development in Italy. Land Use Policy, 64,383–390. https://doi.org/10.1016/j.landusepol.2017.03.002

- ➤ Sonnino, R. (2004). For a 'piece of bread'? Interpreting sustain-able development through agritourism in Southern Tuscany. Sociologia Ruralis,44(3), 285–300. https://doi.org/10.1111/j.1467-9523.2004.00276.x

- ➤ https://keralafarmtourism.com/about-us.html

- ➤ https://www.downtoearth.org.in/tag/economic-survey-2021-2022

CHAPTER 19

KETTUVALLAM TOURISM IN KERALA- AN ENTREPRENEURIAL PARADISE

Sanjith S R
Research scholar
PG Department of Commerce and Research Centre
MG College Thiruvananthapuram, University of Kerala

ABSTRACT

In a contemporary situation central government of India and state government promote self-employment to younger generations through various schemes such as subsidy, loan at lower rate, tax concession, and financial incentives like Mudra loan schemes etc. this is beneficial to the people for starting business enterprises in manufacturing, trading and service sector. Although majority of the entrepreneurs prefers manufacturing sectors and trade for entrepreneurship while a minute entrepreneurs prefer service sector especially in tourism sector. Paradoxically entrepreneurs not as much as prefers tourism sector obviously it is one of the sector demanding high participation of private investment. This is the scenario for recognising an investment avenue in tourism sector called kettuvallam. Kettuvallam is a form of traditional boat in Kerala modified to a private tourism destination owned and operated by private individual with the permission of government. Kettuvallam is an investment avenue where profit as return, creating employment opportunity to residents, introducing cultural values to the rest of the world. Exploiting scenic beauty of backwaters, rivers and estuaries, fish food, flora and fauna, mangrove forest in Kerala etc. are the major attractiveness of kettuvallam tourism. On the basis of geographical specification, Kerala is the most appropriate state of establishing Kettuvallam enterprises. Of course private sector's attention in kettuvallam tourism is highly demanded in the present situation and it is one of the highly emerging investment avenue and highly productive in nature. This study is an attempt to clarify the factors for supporting entrepreneurship in kettuvallam tourism.

Keywords: Kettuvallam, Investment, sustainable Investment Avenue, Entrepreneurship, Tourism, service sector.

INTRODUCTION

Investment is an employment of fund for productive resources with an aim of return. People invested in shares, debentures or bonds, money market instruments, life and general insurance, precious objects, mutual fund, non-marketable securities, derivatives, real estate, Crypto currency etc. with an aim of continuous return. Investment is based on risk taking capacity of investors, expected return, period of investment, liquidity, physical existence, interest, confidence, economic growth and inflation. Majority of an investors prefers any of the above investment alternatives for their safe deposit. In fact there are so many investment avenues are still exist which offers high returns with lowest risk but people have limited idea about such alternatives. Did you ever think individual investment in tourism? Yes it is possible. Majority of the people thinks that tourism is the typical part of government as a whole and people have limited role. Of course in Kerala most of the tourist destinations are directed and controlled by government and allied agencies however there are more scope for private entrepreneurs are still exists.

Kettuvallam is an investment avenue in tourism sector representing commercial property. The person or a group of person or a company who wanted to invest in commercial property and desire to physical existence can prefer kettuvallam as the best investment avenue. Investment in kettuvallam is not at all meant for simple investment, it is a diversified form of investment providing entrepreneurship and employment opportunity to people. Return of investment in Kettuvallam is in the form of profit not interest. Kettuvallam is a cruise boat commonly operated in the lake of Kerala in allied with Tourism department. These are giants boats modified for tourism purpose. During the ancient time kettuvallams are used as a medium of transportation through the inland waterways. Now a day these kettuvallams are modified in to modern houseboats. Such houseboats providing continuous return to the investors and offering employment opportunity to the country residents such craft man, cook, tourist guide etc. Kettuvallam tourism is an emerging tourism sector in the present scenario giving entrepreneurial opportunity to private parties. It is one of the innovative avenue for investment. Investment in Kettuvallam is different from other type of investment because some precautionary procedures have to be accomplished before its operation such as licencing and registration. Licence including Cut number (equal to vehicle number plate for registration) and CIB (Issued by chief inspector of boat)etc. are required for operating a kettuvallam.(Jacob, Kuruvilla, Mahadevan, & Kuruvilla, 2011)[1] in addition to that investment in kettuvallam is an only investment avenue which require certificate from pollution control board.

REVIEW OF LITERATURE

Kettuvallam is a sustainable tourism sector in Kerala offering employability to the local people directly or indirectly. A developing country like India really deserve such type of investment because it offers a platform for investment at the same time it also offers employment opportunity to the community. It's a type of indigenous entrepreneurship which clearly indicating the artwork and craftsmanship of our pioneers. ("Entrepreneurship and Sustainable Tourism: The Houseboats of Kerala—Jithendran Kokkranikal, Alison Morrison, 2002," n.d.)[2].

(Selvakumar, 2011)[3] explains the constructional features of kettuvallam. It is a flat-bottomed, nailed and plank-built boat; intact length ca. 18.67 m, width, ca. 4.05 m. The boat had a transom stern, partly disturbed, and a curvilinear-pointed bow, tied with coir. It does not use a single nail during its manufacturing period. Which resembles kettuvallam. It had double masts, one in the bow and the other amidships. It is made of Anjily wood (Artocarpus hirsutus) and for the bulkhead Cassia fistula wood is used.

(George, 2007)[4] studied the role of cooperative sector in kettuvallam tourism. ATDC (Alleppey Tourism Development Cooperative) which was constituted under the state cooperative Act in 1987 is one of the pioneer harmonised form of society in Alleppey for small and medium term industries. ATDC generally engaged in kettuvallam tourism. Many small scale investors invested in the society for starting for the purpose entrepreneurship. He also states that IT enabled technology can improve the performance of cooperative society as well as marketability of tourism sector.

(Joseph & Vasanthi, n.d.)[5] Houseboat tourism in the backwater of Kerala promote entrepreneurship of local people, contribute to the state and nations. Efficiency of kettuvallam tourism depends on the services offered at kettuvallam, behaviour of employees and marketing strategies of entrepreneurs. Marketability and satisfaction level of tourist can be enhanced through providing proper servicing of the domestic and international tourist as per their needs. Marketing strategies must be designed on the recent trends to create customer values.

(United Nations Conference on Trade and Development, n.d.)[6] express the importance of FDI in tourism sector. It is not only an easy task, While a rigorous segmenting, targeting and positioning approach is a necessary condition for success in promoting inward investment in the tourism industry, it is not sufficient. For inward investment in tourism to be successful, wide-ranging collaboration and coordination between players in the industry – both public and private – is required.

("tourism investment—Google Search," n.d.)[7] Investment in the tourism industry establishes the creation of capital or goods capable of producing other goods or services in tourism industry for earning higher profits in the private sector or regional revitalization or make it as an investment avenue and economic growth for public purposes. When most of the people think of tourism for vacation to a backwater, hill area, farm house, an island, a beautiful vineyard, pilgrims or a mountains and valley. Obviously they rarely think of tourism as a source of inclusive poverty reduction in the developing world. ("Should we be promoting tourism sector investment?," n.d.)[8]

("Travel and Tourism investment expected to rise by 6.7% per annum over next 10 years: FICCI-YES Bank Report—The Economic Times," n.d.)[9] Tourism is one of the fastest growing service industry in India. Approximately 6.7% annual growth rate expected over the next ten years. ("Travel and Tourism Investment in the Americas," n.d.)[10] WTTC has forecast that there will be 3.6 trillion US dollar worth of travel and tourism investment made in the American over the next decade. Which express a strong direct relationship between investment and demand. Which clearly shows the gap between investors in India and America towards investment in tourism.

From the light of review it is clear that investment in tourism sector is highly demanded avenue in the present scenario. According to the report of WTTC developed countries like America already made investment in tourism sector by predicting the future growth in this sector. Even UNCTD promoted FDI in tourism sector. Annual growth rate of Travel and tourism around the globe increases from year to year. A developing country like India expect 6.7% annual growth rate in tourism sector for future decades. People choose destinations of both natural and man-mad tourism according to their need, which clearly indicate tourism is not only for naturally gifted places and it also for the places where tourism is created. This is an occasion for understanding relevance of private investment in tourism sector.

Private investment in tourism sector has greatest opportunity in Kerala. Kettuvallam, amusement parks, statues, parks, farm etc. are the major private tourism products in Kerala. Despite of this fact a few investors chooses tourism sector as Investment Avenue and it is the drawback of tourism sector in Kerala. Detailed study of reviews put forward the problem that "whether entrepreneurial mobility in kettuvallam tourism is beneficial or not in the present scenario?"

OBJECTIVES

> To study the entrepreneurial potential of Kettuvallam tourism in Kerala

METHODOLOGY

This study on kettuvallam tourism an investment avenue analyse the entrepreneurial potentiality of kettuvallam tourism in the state of Kerala. Both primary and secondary data are used for the study. Secondary data collected for building a strong theoretical background about kettuvallam and primary data is collected from kettuvallam entrepreneurs for identifying the existing dilemma and future possibility.

A structured questionnaire is used for collecting primary data from the kettuvallam proprietors. Sampling data collected from 50 kettuvallam entrepreneurs from different destinations such as Alleppey, Kumarakom and Muhamma.

PRODUCT DESIGN-HISTORY OF KETTUVALLAM TOURISM.

Kettuvallam is derived from the word "Kettu" which means tied up and "Vallam" which means boat. As per the names suggest that kettuvallam is a type of boat made up of natural materials such as bamboo, coir, palm wood, palm leaf, plank of jack fruit tree and Aanjili. During the construction of kettuvallam it does not uses any single piece of nail. Coir is used for interconnecting materials hence this name "kettuvallam" derived.

During the ancient period kettuvallam is used for exchanging goods from one place to another through the inland water ways and can carry many tons of goods in a single voyage. Gradually road and rail transportation increases rapidly which reduces the demand of kettuvallam. After some decades some local residents re introduced kettuvallams in a modified form. But this time not for the purpose of goods transportation but for the tourism purpose.

Structure of kettuvallam changes from traditional form of long space to modern form of rooms and sundeck. Interiors were decorated with sophisticated materials and offering high quality services what a three star or five star hotel can offers. The evolution of house boat are as follows.

Figure No-1: Traditional kettuvallam

Source: Secondary data

Figure No-2 : Modern houseboats

Source: secondary data

Figure No-3: Interiors of modern kettuvallam

Source: Secondary data

TYPES OF KETTUVALLAM

Kettuvallam are country boats that were used in ancient days by our pioneers for transport of goods from isolated villages of Kerala backwater area to the towns like Alleppey, Kollam, Cochin and Kottayam. With the advent of land transport facilities, gradually the kettuvallams went off the scene. Now they are back again as a major tourist attraction as a modern moving boat house. They form a huge source of revenue and prosperity for the nation (Mathen, 2012).

Kettuvallam is classified on the basis of facilities they are

1.   Gold star:- deluxe category with less pollution

2.   Silver star:- standard category with less pollution

3.   Green palm:-non-mechanised electric engine with no pollutions.

DATA ANALYSIS

➤   Gender wise classification of Kettuvallam service providers.

Table no-1: Gender

Gender	No of respondents	Percentage
Male	44	88
Female	6	12
Transgender	0	0
Total	50	100

Source: Primary data

Inference: table no -1 shows gender wise classification of kettuvallam service operators. Among the 50 respondents majority of the respondents are male entrepreneurs occupying 88 percentage

➤ Age wise classification of kettuvallam entrepreneurs.

Table no-2: Age

Age	Number of respondents	Percentage
Less than 30	2	4
30-50	15	30
50-70	30	60
Above 70	3	6
Total	50	100

Source: primary data.

Inference: table no-2 represents age wise classification of kettuvallam entrepreneurs. Majority of the kettuvallam entrepreneurs are comes under the age group of 50-70. Only 4 percentage entrepreneurs represent younger generation of less than 30 age category.

➤ Years of experience in kettuvallam operation

Table No-3: Year of experience

Year of Experience	Number of Respondents	Percentage
0-2	6	12
2-5	5	10
5-7	18	36
7-10	8	16
Above 10	13	26
Total	50	100

Source: primary data

Inference: table no-3 reveals that majority of the kettuvallam proprietors are engaged in tourism field from 5 to 7 years, which occupying 36

percentage and 26 percentage of kettuvallam owners has been in this field for more than 10 years.

➤ Classification on the basis of number of kettuvallam owned by entrepreneurs.

Table No-4: Number of houseboat owned

Number of house boat	Number of respondents	Percentage
1	32	64
2	9	18
3	6	12
4	2	4
5 and above	1	2
Total	50	100

Source: primary data

Inference: table number -4 reveals that majority of the entrepreneurs are single owners which represent 64 percentage of the total entrepreneurs. Only 2 percentage owners have more than 5 house boats.

➤ Classification on the basis of types of ownership

Table No -5: Types of ownership

Ownership types	Number of respondents	Percentage
Own	44	88
Rent	3	6
Lease	3	6
Others	0	0
Total	50	100

Source: Primary data

Inference: from table no-5 reveals that majority of the entrepreneurs are real owners which occupy 88 percentage of the total respondents. While 6 percentage of the respondents are operated kettuvallam which has been taken through rental as well as lease basis.

> Classification on the basis of Nature ownership.

Table No-6: Nature of ownership

Nature of ownership	Number of respondents	Percentage	Inference: table number -6 reveals that majority of the respondents are sole proprietors. 70 percentage of the respondents are sole proprietors. 16 percentage of the respondents are doing kettuvallam tourism under partnership basis and 14 percentage of the respondents are doing kettuvallam business as in the form of company.
Sole propri-etorship	35	70	
Partnership	8	16	
Company	7	14	
HUF	0	0	
Cooperative society	0	0	
Total	50	100	

Source: primary data.

> Classification on the basis of primary source of capital

Table No-7: Primary source of capital.

Primary source of capital	Number of respon-dents	Percentage
Own capital	31	62
Loan from financial bank	12	24
Loan from other financial institutions	7	14
Loan from money lenders	0	0
Other sources	0	0
Total	50	100

Source: Primary sources

Inferences: table no 7 reveals that 62 percentage of the respondents uses own finance for initial capital followed by 24 percentage raises fund through loan from bank.

> Factors affecting kettuvallam tourism

Table No-8: Factors affecting kettuvallam tourism

SL No		Financial Factors	Mean	SD
		Volume of initial investment is affordable.	2.64	1.053755
		Source of finance is easily available	2.82	1.071261
		Cost of capital is reasonable	2.46	1.169786
		Floatation cost is modest.	2.66	1.159483
		Operational factors	**Mean**	**SD**
		Wages paid to workers are affordable	3.7	1.374773
i.	Rr	Repair and maintenance expenses are thrifty	2.46	1.268227
		Day to day operational expenses are under budge	4.32	0.988737
		Revenue from tourist are profitable	4.2	1.183216
Registration formalities				
		Registration procedure for kettuvallam is normal	2.94	0.98813
		There is no delay for getting registration certificates.	2.78	1.315903
		License fee charged by the concerned authority is affordable	4.1	0.921954
		Insurance premium amount economical	2.62	1.129425
Marketing factors				
		Functions of concerned Government agencies for tourism development really promote tourism.	3.22	1.005783
		Travel agencies and tour operators facilitates marketing activities	4.02	0.989747
		Unregistered kettuvallam operators does not affect the marketing of registered kettuvallam	1.92	1.09252
		Individual promotional activities increases the marketability of kettuvallam tourism	3.74	1.425623
		Kettuvallam tourism are subjected to modern marketing activities such as social media marketing, internet marketing.	2.58	1.312859
		Kettuvallam operators maintain CRM (Customer Relationship Management)	1.98	0.927146

Source: primary data.

Inferences: 5 point scale is for the responds level of entrepreneurs regarding various factors. Where 5 point is given to highly agreed, 4 point is given to agreed 3 for neither agree nor disagree, 2 for disagree and 1 for highly disagree . The responds level is considered to be disagree if the mean value is less than 3. Highest mean with lowest standard deviation represents the most influenced factors of dependent variables.

On the basis of financial factors four independent variables are analysed. The mean value of all independent financial factor's value are less than 3.which means entrepreneurs have a negative impact on its financial factors such as volume of initial investment, availability of source of finance ,Cost of capital and floatation cost. Among these independent variables availability of source of finance is the most influenced financial factors with highest mean value of 2.82.

On the basis of operational factors entrepreneurs responds that wages paid to workers are affordable ,day to day operational expenses are under budget and revenue from tourist are profitable with mean value more than three that is 3.7, 4.32 and 4.2 respectively. Although entrepreneurs implies that repair and maintenance expense of kettuvallam are unaffordable with mean value 2.46. Among these independent variable day to day expenses of kettuvallam is the most influenced factors which affecting operational factors with highest mean (4.32) and lowest standard deviation (0.988737).

According to the registration formalities of kettuvallam tourism entrepreneurs responds a negative impact with a mean value less than three to the registration formalities, delay in registration certificate and amount of investment premium. However they have positive attitude towards licence fees imposed by the government with mean value more than three (4.1). From the above four factors determining registration factors, license fee is the most influenced factor with highest mean value.

On the basis of marketing factor promotional activity of government, concerned department or government agency, activities of tour operators and travel agency, self-promotion of entrepreneurs etc. are the most influenced factors of marketing of kettuvallam tourism. Even though marketing activities of tour operators and travel agency plays a vital role among these factors with a mean value of 4.02. Despite the fact that lower performance in CRM is the highly negative factor in marketing of kettuvallam tourism with lowest mean value of 1.98.

Figure No-4: Recommendation to incubators

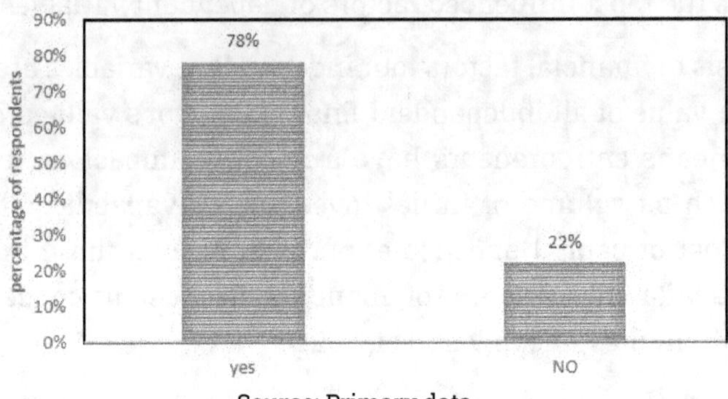

Source: Primary data

Inference: figure no 4 explains that majority of the existing entrepreneurs recommend kettuvallam business to the upcoming entrepreneurs.

FINDINGS

1. Majority of the kettuvallam entrepreneurs are male.

2. Majority of the kettuvallam entrepreneurs are comes under the age group of 60-70.

3. Majority of the kettuvallam entrepreneurs are engaged in the field of kettuvallam tourism from 5 to 7 years followed by people with more than 10 years' experience which clearly indicate that the profitability in long run.

4. Majority of the entrepreneurs have only one kettuvallam. And uses own fund for the construction and renovation of the cruise ship.

5. Sole proprietor is the common form of entrepreneur in the field of kettuvallam. And majority of the entrepreneur's using own kettuvallam than rental and lease.

6. Financial factors tends to have a negative approach in entrepreneurs of kettuvallam due to huge capital investment and source of finance. Which express that Kettuvallam is not suitable under the category of micro business. It is suitable to small and medium term enterprises.

7. Entrepreneurs have negative approach on repair and maintenance expenses of kettuvallam, insurance premium and its registration formalities. Although entrepreneurs satisfied with licence fees.

8. Activities of tour operators are the major marketing factor in kettuvallam tourism than individual promotion and promotion of government agencies.

9. Problem of poor CRM exist.

10. Majority of the entrepreneurs recommend kettuvallam as an investment avenue for entrepreneurship to the upcoming entrepreneurs.

SUGGESTIONS

1. Promote women entrepreneurs to the kettuvallam tourism

2. Simplify registration procedures and could take measures for avoiding the delay in supply of registration certificates.

3. Promote younger generation to the kettuvallam tourism through various schemes and policies.

4. If kettuvallam tourism is included in MSME it could be more beneficial to the incubators.

5. Marketing become more powerful if entrepreneurs take initiative steps for implementing CRM

CONCLUSION

Investment in tourism sector not only mean for steady return it is also a business and profit as the return. Moreover it create employment opportunity to the local people, craft man, fisherman etc. Investment in kettuvallam for the purpose of starting a new ventures is a highly potential business in now a days. Younger generation and women entrepreneurs have lot of opportunity in kettuvallam tourism. However some limitations are existed in this business like any other business such huge capital, marketing problem and seasonal variation. Although these are avoidable with effective planning and control mechanism.

REFERENCES

➤ Jacob, R., Kuruvilla, A., Mahadevan, P., & Kuruvilla, A. (2011). PRODUCT ATTRACTIVENESS OF KERALA HOUSE BOATS IN PROMOTING TOURISM-A PERFORMANCE ANALYSIS. THE INTERNATIONAL SOUNDS AND TASTES OF TOURISM EDUCATION, 63.

➤ Entrepreneurship and Sustainable Tourism: The Houseboats of Kerala—Jithendran

Kokkranikal, Alison Morrison, 2002. (n.d.). Retrieved November 20, 2019, from https://journals.sagepub.com/doi/abs/10.1177/146735840200400102

➤ Selvakumar, V. (2011). Archaeological, Literary and Ethnographic Evidence for Traditional Boat-building in Kerala, South India. Asia-Pacific Regional Conference on Underwater Cultural Heritage, November 2011.

➤ George, B. P. (2007). Alleppey tourism development cooperative: The case of network advantage. The Public Sector Innovation Journal, 12(2), 1–10.

➤ Joseph, L. C., & Vasanthi, S. (n.d.). A STUDY ON MOTIVATING FACTORS OF THE TOURISTS ABOUT THE HOUSE BOATS SERVICES IN KUMARAKOM, ALEPPEY DISTRICT.

➤ United Nations Conference on Trade and Development. (n.d.). Promoting foreign investment in tourism. 78.

➤ Should we be promoting tourism sector investment? (n.d.). Retrieved December 13, 2019, from World Bank Blogs website: https://blogs.worldbank.org/psd/should-we-be-promoting-tourism-sector-investment

➤ tourism investment—Google Search. (n.d.). Retrieved December 13, 2019, from https://www.google.com/search?q=tourism+investment&rlz=1C1CHBF_

CHAPTER 20

"A STUDY ON SATISFACTION LEVEL OF TOURISTS' TOWARDS AYURVEDA TOURISM IN KERALA"

Athira K. A.
Lecturer at MGM College
of Arts and Science
Kaniyapuram Trivandrum

ABSTRACT

India is considered as one of the most popular tourist destinations in the world. Tourism plays a critical role in country's economic growth and prosperity. Kerala is a popular tourist destination because of its culture and traditional medical systems like ayurveda. Medical tourism is a subset of health tourism which is an emerging trend in Kerala. Tourist preference to visit a particular destination will always depends on the quality of services provided at tourist destination. Kerala is well known for its ayurveda tourism. The quality of services provided at the ayurveda tourist spots makes it more fruitful and gives better experience for the tourists. Kerala has became the hot spot for the ayurvedic treatments and popular for its rejuvenation therapies. As Kerala is an important destination for ayurveda tourism, it fosters development of overall tourism sector in Kerala and increases revenue too. This study focuses on finding the level of satisfaction among tourists towards ayurveda tourism in Kerala.

Keywords: Tourist satisfaction, Ayurveda tourism, Kerala, Traditional medical systems, culture.

INTRODUCTION:

In India, Tourism is considered as an important sector which has gone through different developments phases. Under this sector health tourism has gained its special attraction among the tourists worldwide. It has attracted many foreigners towards India. Kerala is the brand ambassador of Ayurveda tourism in India. The services provided by Kerala and its eco-friendly approach are the main reason for the flow of tourists. Ayurveda is generally a treatment of relaxation of not only body but also mind. It has medicines for almost all the diseases and large number of people depends on it. Ayurveda has huge untapped potential which must be utilised to treatment many lifestyle diseases. Central, state, and local governments are taking necessary steps to promote the ayurvedic tourism all over the world. They are supporting this sector by imparting knowledge about its advantages and by the way attracting large number of people towards ayurveda tourism. Kerala ayurveda tourism sector has become an important tourism during the past two decades. By promoting the ayurveda treatments Kerala has achieved about 30% increase in its tourist flow and an increase in 40 % revenue flow towards the state.

REVIEW OF LITERATURE

(UNCTAD, 2010): Tourism sector has emerged as one of the devices of economic development, poverty alleviation, employment generation and sustainable human development. Tourism has become the second largest net foreign exchange earner for the country. "Tourism Sector is a major generator of employment.

As a highly labor intensive activity, tourism and tourism support activities create a high proportion of employment and career opportunities for low skilled and semi-skilled workers, particularly for poor, female and young workers. Women make up 70 percent of the labor force in tourism sector and half of all tourism workers are 25 years or under. The tourism sector can be an important source of employment for many of the unemployed youth and consequently reduces the poverty in the society"

Jaiswal and Williams, Yoginiet (2017) opined Ayurveda, most popular way of treatment from ancient India is persisted and succeeded from past to present. Here the authors try to enrich the history of Ayurveda which include the role of Ayurveda in different periods. We get knowledge about vedas, Pancha Mahabhootas, tridoshas, Pancha Karma and other related activities..

Varghese and Zacharias (2020) found out that vital strategy for attracting the patients from abroad is on line communication and the clients also rely on the information received from on line transactions.

Louis (2018) there were substantial connotation amongst the satisfaction level and the essentials connected to it and Kerala has ample resources for attracting the world as it is the brand ambassador of Ayuevedic sector.

Bulsara and Yadav (2018) Users are nowadays practical oriented and they understand that Ayurveda the traditional medicine treat the body as a whole rather than quick relief but rarely people use modern medicine in critical situations

Acharyya (2020) explained that Ayurveda has enough opportunities as a precautionary measure for fighting against COVID 19 pandemic. In order to practice ayurveda as restorative and deterrent facet scientific studies associated with it and its principles are desirable. WHO also recommended these types of activities at the time of epidemic diseases.

SIGNIFICANCE OF THE STUDY:

Kerala is the most important destination for health tourism in Kerala especially ayurveda. It gives lifelong relief to diseases, also gives relaxation to body and mind. It is the core reason for the attraction of more tourists towards Kerala every year. As far as Kerala is concerned, it is important to provide better quality experience to their tourists to attract more in future. The tourist loyalty will always depend on the satisfaction level of the tourists. This study aims at finding the level of tourist satisfaction towards ayurvedic tourism. This would probably give solutions to the major problems that make the tourists unsatisfied.

SCOPE OF THE STUDY:

In Kerala, Thiruvananthapuram and Ernakulam districts has a large number of tourist visits for ayurvedic treatment. Eco friendly environment, transportation facilities, quality food and accommodation, native culture with hospitality and the real ayurvedic services attracts more foreign and domestic tourists to Kerala. So, the scope of the study is limited to Thiruvananthapuram and Ernakulam districts in Kerala.

OBJECTIVES OF THE STUDY

In the view of the above introductory area, the following objectives have been laid down:

1. To find out the level of satisfaction among the tourists towards

ayurvetic tourism in Kerala

2. To understand necessary steps to be taken to improve the ayurvedic tourism in Kerala.

THEORETICAL FRAMEWORK

SCOPE OF AYURVEDIC TOURSIM

Ayurvedic tourism in Kerala has got its own scope for development and attracting tourists. But due to several reasons its importance are not recognized and supported. The reasons are the followings:

1. **LACK OF AWARENESS:**

People in and around India are still not aware about the importance of ayurveda. There are no proper initiatives taken from the part of government to spread the knowledge about ayurveda. People still believe that only allopathic medicines has got the power to sure any disease.

2. **FALIURE IN PROVIDING SERVICES TO POOR:**

 Ayurvedic treatments in Kerala are less affordable to poor people and this is another reason for lack of development of ayurvedic tourism.

SUPPORT FROM GOVERNMENT:

Government has implemented new policies and programmes to support the ayurvedic tourism in Kerala. The government ayurvedic hospitals give more care to poor in and outside the state. In the last two decades there is a gradual increase in the number of tourists visiting Kerala for ayurvedic treatments. Government organized promotional activities and provided a better experience for all the tourists visiting for the ayurvedic treatments. By this way, Kerala has achieved about 30% increase in its tourist flow and an increase in 40 % revenue flow towards the state.

FOREIGN TOURIST VISIT TO KERALA

YEAR	NO OF FOREIGN TOURISTS VISITED	% VARIATION OVER PY	FOREIGN EXCHANGE EARINGS	% VARIATION OVER PY

2018	1096407	0.42%	8764.46	4.44%
2017	1091870	-	8392.11	-

DOMESTIC TOURIST VISIT TO KERALA

YEAR	NO OF DOMESTIC TOURISTS VISITED	% VARIATION OVER PY	FOREIGN EXCHANGE EARINGS	% VARIATION OVER PY
2018	15604661	6.35%	36258.01	8.61%
2017	14673520		33383.68	

It is understood from the above Kerala tourism visit in the years 2018 and 2017 that, there is a gradual increase in the visit of tourists to Kerala. And also there is an increase in the revenue to the health tourism sector. In 2019, Kerala faced natural calamities like flood, which has negatively affected the overall tourist sector. But still enormous number of tourists arrived to Kerala in 2019 which include domestic -18384233 and foreign -1189771. The percentage of growth was 17.8% in domestic tourists and 8.5% in foreign tourists.

TOURIST SATISFACTION AND TOURIST LOYALTY:

Kerala is considered as one of the most popular destinations in the world because of its culture and traditions. The tag line "Kerala- God's own country" was adopted to promote tourism in all over the world.As far as tourism is concerned; the most important thing is tourist loyalty. Frequent and repeated visit to the same spot by the tourists paves way for development of tourism sector. Destination loyalty is the term closely related to tourist's satisfaction. When tourists are provided with better services and tourist experience, they become more loyal and satisfied. Destination loyalty is the major outcome of a quality delivery of tourist services. The critical linkages of destination loyalty includes brand image of physical environment, people friendliness and kindness. Tourist is said to have loyalty to the destination only when the reality matches or goes above the expectations which is simply called satisfaction.

In ayurvedic tourism, tourists must be satisfied with services of hospitals, clinic, physician and others externals things like easy arrival to India etc...The tourists must be provided with best treatments, medicines and better physical environment.

1. **BEST SERVICES:** The tourists must be provided with better care and services. All their requirements must be fulfilled and they should be given an overall better experience.

2. **BEST FACILITIES:** The tourists must be provided with best facilities like good hospital environment, food, accommodation, clean drinking water etc.

3. **QUALITY TREATMENT**: It is the responsibility of the physician to provide best treatment the tourists.

4. **HOSPITALITY:** More tourists are attracted to ayurvedic tourism only when they are satisfied with the hospitality provided.

5. **REASONABLE CHARGE:** The overall ayurvedic treatment must be charged at reasonable rate, since it has a huge impact on further arrival of tourists to same spot.

6. **RELAXATION OF BODY AND MIND**: Most of the ayurvedic tourists visiting Kerala is are aimed at getting their body and mind relaxed. This treatment in Kerala has worldwide recognition and attracts large number of tourist from in and outside India.

FINDINGS

From the data gathered with the help of secondary sources, the following findings are collected:

1. Tourists are highly satisfied with the hospital services like better treatment, clean atmosphere etc...

2. Tourists are satisfied the food and accommodation provided at the destination.

3. Tourists are having a positive feedback towards the confirmation of appointments in destination

4. They are happy that there were no complicated procedures for getting

visa to arrive India.

5. Most of the tourists are happy with overall services provided and are satisfied.

6. Some tourists faced some problems related to high cost for the ayurvedic treatments in some destinations in Kerala.

SUGGESTIONS:

1. Government has to take steps to provide more ayurvedic destinations in Kerala.

2. Government has to organize awareness programs relating to the importance of ayurveda.

3. More tourists can be attracted to ayurvedic tourism by the way of increasing publicity and promotion.

4. Tourists can be provided with even better treatments at reasonable costs.

CONCLUSION:

Kerala ayurveda tourism sector has become an important tourism during the past two decades. By promoting the ayurveda treatments Kerala has achieved about 30% increase in its tourist flow and an increase in 40 % revenue flow towards the state. . The tag line "Kerala- God's own country" was adopted to promote tourism in all over the world.As far as tourism is concerned; the most important thing is tourist loyalty. Frequent and repeated visit to the same spot by the tourists paves way for development of tourism sector.

The ayurveda treatment is considered as the most popular treatment for relaxation of mind and body. More tourists are attracted towards this due to these reasons. Kerala is well known for its services to tourists. So, it can be concluded that Kerala's ayurvedic tourism is attract large number of people in and around India because of its better quality services and making its customers satisfied.

REFERENCES:

➤ Chawla Romila(2010)Sarjeet Publishers, Tourist Marketing And Communication pp 130-148.

➤ Ahmed, Acharyya, A. (2020). Prospect of Ayurveda System of Medicine in recent COVID-19 Pandemic in India . International Journal of Ayurveda and Traditional Medicine, 2(2), 26-29

➤ Bulsara, H. P., & Yadav, N. (2018). Study On The Current Scenario Of Consumers Buying Behavior Towards Ayurvedic Medicines In Gujarat. IOSR Journal of Business and Management , 31-35

➤ G, H. N. (2005). "Study of the application of information technology in the treatment and preparation of medicine in ayurveda with special reference to Kerala". Calicut: University of Calicut.

➤ T, B. V., & Swain, S. K. (2012). A Study on Destination Image of Kerala as an Ayurvedic Healthcare Destination. Asia Joural of Transfusion Science, 7 (1), 45-58.

➤ Agnives, C. R. (2002). Development of Ayurveda through Ages. (pp. 1-5). Kochi: Swadeshi Science Movement,

CHAPTER 21

VILLAGE TOURISM IN INDIA

Dr. Tajinder Kaur
Assistant Professor
Department of Commerce
Post Graduate Government College
Sector-46, Chandigarh

ABSTRACT

India, being the second largest country in terms of population and still a developing country, is having many problems. For its development it requires to improve its spending on education, skill development and making its population employable. Village tourism is one aspect through which it can give employment to villagers and make them self-sufficient. India is a country where there is vast potential for village tourism. The states differ in its geographical conditions, languages, art, and culture. Some of the states attract tourism like, Rajasthan, Gujarat, Delhi, Uttar Pradesh, Kerala, Uttarakhand, Himachal Pradesh etc. They not only attract Indian tourist but they also attract foreign tourists. On the same pattern village tourism can be promoted not only for tourism in India but also for foreigners. The paper studies the different ways how village tourism can be promoted and how India can solve its problem of unemployment.

Key words: Tourism, Earnings, Employability, Art and Culture, NEP

INTRODUCTION

Tourism is also an industry which provides livelihood to many people. It can be taken as an opportunity in Indian villages to promote tourism. Lessons can be learned from states which attract international tourists and promote their art and culture. They promote their art and culture, provide good facilities for staying. Around 65% population of India is living in villages in the year 2020 (Data from World Bank). They primarily rely on agriculture for their living. Village tourism will provide them with work, promote art and culture, and help in the development of the village. Various problems in India can be solved by local innovations. That can be done when students and researchers will be given the opportunity to live in the village and study its life. Village tourism will also help in including women in the workforce as they are confined to local areas and are relatively less literate. There are different ways through which village tourism can be promoted. For such promotion governments at state level can frame plans by initially developing model villages. Then after, more villages can be attached to this concept. The government of India has introduced the concept of model villages where an MP would have to adopt a village and develop it. Development in terms of health, infrastructure nutrition and education will provide a basis for the development of village tourism.

FOCUSING ON THE ART AND CULTURE OF THE VILLAGE

In every state there are many villages. Their art and culture differs from village to village. To promote village tourism, art and culture can be used as a major factor to attract tourists. In selected villages tourist spots can be developed. At tourist spots, cultural items can be displayed. It will give employment to villagers and memorable experience to the tourists.

SAFE RESIDENTIAL PLACES FOR TOURISTS

In villages, if a person is interested to spend few days there is problem of staying in the village, cleanliness etc. but if the village tourism is promoted then common residences can be built where good facilities will be provided to the tourists to spend their time and enjoy the life of the village. It will provide safety to tourists and will generate income for the owners of those properties. It will attract tourists internationally and also locally.

PROJECT ON VILLAGE FOR STUDENTS

Villages are places where one can feel fresh air and fresh food. But it also faces many problems. Its solution can be done by educated villagers or by young students. In the curriculum of school and colleges on assignment can be given on study of village life. They can spend their time, can have experience of village life, and can make assignments to solve the various problems through their ideas. If the villages will provide safe residential space to the outsiders by providing them facilities, not only they can earn income but they also will be able to give opportunity to others to know about village life. This will make school children more confident and will help them to know their country better.

FOCUS ON DRESSES AND EATING'S

Every state has its own dressing sense and dishes to eat. Village tourism will provide them opportunity to sell their products and earn. As in Rajasthan, its local festivals are celebrated and are the main centre of attraction for foreigners in the similar way Indian villages can be projected. That will keep its culture alive and will provide experience to others.

VILLAGE FARMING

Villages are known for its farming and that can be used as an attraction centre for the tourist. Through tourism they can be given a chance to enjoy the process of farming. They can even contribute to village farming. It will help them to understand how the different crops are grown. They can also enjoy the freshness and fresh food of the village.

FILM ON VILLAGE LIFE

To promote villages in tourism, a film making competition can be organised on yearly basis. Participant will make film on village life. It will give chance to the film makers to spend time in the village and rich heritage and culture of the village can be preserved. This also will promote villagers to come forward in film making. Yearly completion of such an event will help in bringing out the best in the villages.

EVENT MANAGEMENT

Event management is one of the ways how one can earn by just managing the event. Event can be a marriage party, get together, birthday party, and other business events. Villages' tourism can add event organization which can give the feel of fresh food and village-specific culture to the parties. Many people feel like moving out of towns to live and enjoy a different life which is full of peace. Such events can help them to enjoy their life.

CELEBRATION OF FESTIVALS SPECIFIC OF THAT STATE

India is a country with vast cultural diversity. Each state is rich in its geographical location, culture, language, festivals etc. giving feel of the celebration of festivals in villages can be a unique idea for village tourism. People from different states can go to the village festival and can enjoy the culture of that place. It will generate revenue for the villagers.

SCIENCE MUSEUMS IN VILLAGES

To promote education in the field of science, it is important that students can gain knowledge about it through museums. At small levels, science museums can be made in model villages so that knowledge about science can be gained by villagers and can be used by tourists when they visit the village. When school children are given the opportunity to live in the village, they can spend their time on productive work.

POINT FOR BUSINESS IDEAS

Villagers are generally very much contented in their life; they lack investment to begin any business. Point of business ideas can attract investors and can provide business opportunity to the villagers. To attract investors, some model villages in each state can be developed and investors interested in rural customers can be invited to check the business potential in the village. Regular meetings and discussions will bring market of products made in the villages. It also will provide a market for different investors. These ideas will attract investors through the concept of village tourism.

VILLAGE LITERATURE FEST

The national Education Policy emphasizes the development of local languages to keep it alive and save it from extinction. Literature fests in the villages can promote the contribution of villagers in their in their literature. It will also promote writing skills among the localized, then all such knowledge and literary items can be displayed on the websites of the respective states. It will attract researchers working on languages to get the information required. This also will attract academicians to the villages.

CONCLUSION

The development of villages is directly related to village tourism. It not only preserves the art and culture of the village but also will provide employment to the population residing in villages. India has not developed fully its village tourism. By developing model villages, organizing village literature fest, event management, point of business idea, etc. will promote local language, art, and culture of the village.

With our own innovation and workforce, the problems of villages can be solved. India can take advantage of its rich culture, geographically different environment, healthy food etc. through village tourism. It will be beneficial not only to the villagers but also to the whole nation.

REFERENCES

- https://data.worldbank.org/indicator/SP.RUR.TOTL.ZS?locations=IN (as on 3-1-2022)
- https://www.sciencedirect.com/science/article/abs/pii/S221197361200013X (as on 2-1-2022)
- https://www.sciencedirect.com/science/article/abs/pii/S0261517797000344 (as on 2-1-2022)
- https://ncert.nic.in/textbook/pdf/keec106.pdf (as on 3-1-2022)

CHAPTER 22

INNOVATIVE BANKING STRATEGIES –AN OVERVIEW

Dr. Saleena A.S.
Assistant Professor of Commerce,
Iqbal College, Peringammala, University of Kerala.

ABSTRACT

The banking system in India is undergoing structural transformation under the influence of globalization, deregulation, technological advances and institutional and legal reforms. The study sought to identify the strategies adopted by banks in India and reviewed innovation, technology competence as the key independent variables for tourism progress. Technological innovations, but fierce competition and changing purchasing behaviour of the beneficiaries of banking services and products banks have challenged management, directing their work towards introduction of modern technologies to promote banking products and services. Adapting to new technologies and innovations in the banking field needs is strategic for any financial institution that aimed at both retail and corporate activity which leads to improved operative staff, by targeting the growing activities of guidance, coordination and advice to clients in tourism scenario.

Keywords: Innovation, technology, tourism, banking products.

INTRODUCTION

In recent years, the banking industry around the world has been undergoing a rapid transformation. In India also, the wave of deregulation of early 1990s has created heightened competition and greater risk for banks and other financial intermediaries. The cross-border flows and entry of new players and products have forced banks to adjust the product-mix and undertake rapid changes in their processes and operations to remain competitive. The deepening of technology has facilitated better tracking and fulfilment of commitments, multiple delivery channels for customers and faster resolution of mis coordination's. Unlike in the past, the banks today are market driven and market responsive. Innovation in any Industry or Department needs basic organizational support to succeed. The same holds true for the Banking Sector too. Today the banking sector is facing multiple pressures. On the one hand, banks have to adapt to greater regulation, competition and consolidation, which are largely out of their control; on the other, they have to meet increasingly diverse and demanding customer expectations. Most realize that innovation is indispensable to their future growth and sustainability. Those with serious innovation intent must give it the best chance of success by laying the requisite groundwork. Historically, banks have innovated at a slower pace compared to many other businesses. Regulation and risk mitigation has as much to do with this as the fact that the results of innovation take time to show, giving competitors a chance to match or even better a pioneering effort. Innovation is perceived as the key to growth and competitive differentiation. Corporate and retail banks today are facing competition from new entrants and innovative business models.

Banking is an epicentre of economic development and sound Management is the basic need to create confidence and accelerate the process of economic growth. The banking system in India is undergoing structural transformation under the influence of globalization, deregulation, technological advances and institutional and legal reforms. Technological innovations, but fierce competition and changing purchasing behaviour of the beneficiaries of banking services and products have challenged management, directing their work towards introduction of modern technologies to promote banking products and services. Adapting to new technologies and innovations in the field is strategic for any financial institution aimed at both retail and corporate activity which leads to improved operative staff, by targeting the growing activities of guidance, coordination and advice to clients. Technology innovations, fierce competition and changing purchasing behaviour of the beneficiaries of banking services and products have challenged management, directing their work towards introduction of modern technologies to promote banking products and services. Adapting to new technologies and innovations in the field need strategic analysis for any financial institution aimed at both retail and corporate activity which leads to improved operative staff, by targeting the growing activities of guidance, coordination and advice to clients. The tempo of development for the Indian banking industry has been remarkable over the past decade. It is evident from the higher pace of credit expansion; expanding profitability and productivity similar to banks in developed markets, lower incidence of non- performing assets and focus on financial inclusion have contributed to making Indian banking vibrant and strong. Indian banks have begun to revise their growth approach and re-evaluate the prospects on hand to keep the economy rolling.

RESEARCH OBJECTIVE & METHODOLOGY

The major objective of this study is to gain insights into innovative strategies adopted by banks in the last couple of years that lead to tourism progress. The research has been carried out, primarily by interacting with a few banking professionals and, secondarily, through Review of Literature, Published Journals, Data Sources and thorough study of examination of research articles.

RECENT CHANGES IN INDIAN BANKING SECTOR

1.   Internet banking

The shift towards internet banking is fuelled by the changing dynamics in India. By 2020, the average age of India will be 29 years and this young consumer base is internet savvy and wants real time online information. Indian banks therefore need to aspire high and move toward implementing a world class internet banking capability Urban areas had a total of 205 million internet users in October 2013 that accounts for 40% growth, while rural India have 68 million users and a growth rate of 58%.

2. Business intelligence

India's banking industry is on the cusp of a major transformation, with new banking licenses expected to bring in more players in an already competitive environment. In such an environment, banks across India are increasingly adopting business intelligence (BI) and analytics to drive their overall profitability.RBI has also encouraged banks to adopt BI to increase transparency and control over the banking business. The Automated Data Flow (ADF) initiative has been a strategic step in this direction, seeking to ensure submission of correct and consistent data from banks' systems to the RBI without any manual intervention.

3. IT in Banking

Indian banking industry, today is in the midst of an IT revolution. A combination of regulatory and competitive reasons has led to increasing importance of total banking automation in the Indian Banking Industry. The bank which used the right technology to supply timely information will see productivity increase and thereby gain a competitive. To compete in an economy which is opening up, it is imperative for the Indian Banks to observe the latest technology and modify it to suit their environment. Information technology offers a chance for banks to build new systems that address a wide range of customer needs including many that may not be imaginable today. Nowadays we are hearing about e-governance, e-mail, e-commerce, e-tail etc. In the same manner, a new technology is being developed in US for introduction of e-cheque, which will eventually replace the conventional paper-cheque. India, as harbinger to the introduction of e-cheque, the Negotiable Instruments Act has already been amended to include; Truncated cheque and E-cheque instruments.

4. Real Time Gross Settlement (RTGS)

Real Time Gross Settlement system, introduced in India since March 2004, is a system through which electronics instructions can be given by banks to transfer funds from their account to the account of another bank. The RTGS system is maintained and operated by the RBI and provides a means of efficient and faster funds transfer among banks facilitating their financial operations. As the name suggests, funds transfer between banks takes place on a 'Real Time' basis. Therefore, money can reach the beneficiary instantaneously and the beneficiary's bank has the responsibility to credit the beneficiary's account within two hours.

5. Electronic Funds Transfer (EFT)

Electronic Funds Transfer (EFT) is a system whereby anyone who wants to make payment to another person/company etc. can approach his bank and make cash payment or give Instructions/authorization to transfer funds directly from his own account to the bank account of the receiver/ beneficiary. Complete details such as the receiver's name, bank account Number, account type (savings or current account), bank name, city, branch name etc. should be furnished to the bank at the time of requesting for such transfers so that the amount reaches the beneficiaries' account correctly and faster. RBI is the service provider of EFT.

6. Automatic Teller Mach (ATM)

Automatic Teller Machine is the most popular devise in India, which enables the customers to withdraw their money 24 hours a day 7 days a week. It is a device that allows customer who has an ATM card to perform routine banking transactions without interacting with a human teller. In addition to cash withdrawal, ATMs can be used for payment of utility bills, funds transfer between accounts, deposit of cheques and cash into accounts, balance enquiry etc.

7. Tele Banking

Tele Banking facilitates the customer to do entire non-cash related banking on telephone. Under this devise Automatic Voice Recorder is used for simpler queries and transactions. For complicated queries and transactions, manned phone terminals are used.

8. Electronic Data Interchange (EDI)

Electronic Data Interchange is the electronic exchange of business documents like purchase order, invoices, shipping notices, receiving advices etc. in a standard, computer processed, universally accepted format between trading partners. EDI can also be used to transmit financial information and payments in electronic form.

INNOVATIVE BANK MARKETING IN A COMPETITIVE ENVIRONMENT

As the United States of America emerges from financial crisis, retail banks are striving to outperform their competitors while haplessly grappling with unprecedented regulatory challenges and shifts in customer behaviour. Today's retail banks are operating in a new banking environment. Today's need of the hour, banking leaders need to quickly and decisively adopt new approaches or simply face the risk of being left behind. Banks, in the current scenario will need to formulate their strategies in the midst of unprecedented changes. These could be:

Change in the way banking platforms are adopted: – Leading institutions are adopting a new customer-centric model to replace outdated product-centric models. In my view, banks should focus on gaining their customers' trust by identifying and addressing customers' overall financial goals, then deliver products and services to help achieve those goals. Each customer should be assigned an advocate within the bank, popularly known as Relationship Manager whose job should be to identify and manage the customer's long-term financial goals and guide to relevant products and services. Loyalty programs, if in place, should be promoted in rewarding customers for activities undertaken across multiple product lines. This is the right time now for banks to replace age old legacy of core banking platforms. This is because, aging, non integrated legacy banking systems are becoming a liability, as maintenance costs rise and customers demand real-time access to information and services. There has to be a paradigm change in which the customer is served and thus should be left with no post purchase dissonance.

Changing consumer behaviours and expectations—An Indian consumer today is striving to save more, spend less, and bring down his liability of debt. Consumer satisfaction levels are on the decline—and the emergence of social media has created a new source of publicity with which banks have to comply with. In a customer-centric model, features have to be designed to improve the customer experience. The customer's information should be integrated and can be accessed from any location. The customer should not be required to complete redundant forms, which speeds processing and improves the customer experience. There has to be single credit underwriting process, even for customers who have multiple loans with the bank.

Mobile technology and social media—The explosive growth of Smartphone technology has created a new distribution channel. Banks today boast of advanced mobile strategy—and it's not just a matter of making online banking available on a smaller device, it is reaching out to every nook and corner of the country at just a click of a button. With the advent of social media, customers are now sharing their experiences in real time. The social media explosion requires companies to monitor what is being said about them and to take advantage of this channel to build loyal advocates. Social media provides banks with a new way to improve brand recognition, expand customer reach, enhance the customer experience, and introduce new products.

Industry consolidation - Government-assisted deals continue to provide banks with a unique opportunity to gain market share. The winners will be the banks that can successfully make the whole greater than the sum of their parts and build loyalty with new customers for years to come. The banking industry is under pressure in today's business climate. Banks have been through extensive changes. There is opportunity, but there is also increasing competition. To be the preferred bank means changing "good enough" into a unique value proposition. And that means changing the way people have always done things.

Changing Technology in Banking- Innovations in information and communication technology are perceived to be the important factor for productivity and growth. The relationship between IT and Banking is fundamentally high thanks to the innovations in the field of IT and communications. This has led to drastic reduction in costs, increased volumes and facilitation of customized products. Public sector must adopt the changing technology in order to compete with Private and Public sector banks. Most importantly, the retention of customers can be made only through adoption of new technology like ATMs, telephone banking, On-line bill payment and Internet banking.

Financial Inclusion: On Independence Day 2014, India's Prime Minister Narendra Modi launched his financial inclusion plan to provide a bank account to every Indian household. His 'Jan-Dhan Yojna' (Scheme for People's Wealth) seeks to provide financial independence to unbanked Indians. It focuses on providing every household in India with a free zero-balance bank account and a RuPay debit card — which allows for electronic payment at all Indian banks — with an aim of increasing financial literacy among the poor. Account holders will also receive up to Rs 100,000 of accident insurance and an overdraft of Rs 5000 after six months. India is on the path to becoming a cashless society. Prime Minister Modi's Jan-Dhan Yojna is one more step towards a more developed India nd possibly a big step — if successful.

PENETRATING RURAL AREAS

As rural population is scattered in small villages having branches few kilo meters away, it's difficult for them to reach bank regularly as its time consuming for them. Here Public sector banks have come up with innovative ideas of Micro Branch or Branchless Banking. Public sector banks are far ahead of Private Banks in penetrating in these remote areas. Beside this the latest "Jan Dhan Yojna" has also boosted Public sector banks in rural areas to get maximum new accounts. (Savings)

CONVERGENCE OF MOBILE AND ONLINE TECHNOLOGIES

Mobile banking started as a novelty, something only techies and first adopters felt comfortable using. But as smart phones have skyrocketed in popularity over the past few years, mobile banking adoption has increased along with it."Mobile banking became a much known phenomena, familiar to known maximum as it very much an offshoot of the online channel."

THE RISE OF BUSINESS PROCESS MANAGEMENT

Both to increase efficiency and ensure regulatory compliance, banks need better methods of gathering and reporting data. Most banks struggle with multiple backoffice systems and confidential information. To address these issues in earnest, there will be a large investment in new improved business process management tools in the year head.

GOODBYE EMAIL, HELLO MESSAGE CENTRE

The abandonment of email for anything sensitive already has began and the shift has been made to the total reliance on message centre. This is a search by portals designed for secure communication between a bank and its customers.

THE 'TABULARIZATION' OF BANKING AND THE USER EXPERIENCE

Tablet banking is still a young channel, but it is needed with full potential. As with initial mobile forays, it may take banks some period of trial and error to determine how to build the best banking experience for the environment. But most experts agree that the potential for a great banking use experience which is unlimited in use.

REACHING THE NEXT LEVEL OF MOBILE EVOLUTION

Mobile banking and payments saw major growth in 2013-14 from tech companies and financial institutions launching mobile wallets to consumers utilizing a mobile application to buy a cup of coffee. But 2015 will be the year in which mobile finance gains strategic direction, and banks will introduce next-generation mobile initiatives to drive balance sheet impacts.

CONCLUSION

Banking sector is the most extensively regulated sector in Indian financial market. Bank systems and technology identifies the IT trends and recent technologies that will change the game in the year ahead. "Still in its early stages, banks also report seeing mobile phones as a powerful marketing channel letting them make offers directly to individual customers at a particular time and place." Moreover, as Indian banks are the catalysts of the inclusive growth of the economy it is advisable to adopt the new concept of reporting because of its consequences benefits for nation's interest thereby boosting the tourism environment.

BIBLIOGRAPHY

➤ Indian Banking 2020 Report September 2010 by bcg.com

➤ Opportunities & Challenges of Indian Financial Markets Report By PwC India

➤ Reimagining Banking in India 2013 Report by McKinsey & Company, Inc.

➤ Indian Banking Industry: Challenges And Opportunities International Journal of

➤ Application or Innovation in Engineering & Management (IJAIEM) Volume 2, Issue

   1, January 2013 ISSN 2319 -4847

➤ Wikipedia.com

CHAPTER 23

DREAM CATCHER @ A COFFEE SHOP

Dr. M.S.Gayathri Devi
Assistant Professor, Department of English,
Mahatma Gandhi College, Trivandrum.

ABSTRACT

The paper highlights in detail the therapeutic effect that travel, whether long or short, can bring to an individual. Through a memory sequence it discusses in detail how it affects the overall persona of an individual, which add on as small small happiness leading to a healthy mental state.

Key Words: Psyche, Hedonism, Eudemonism, Subjective well being, Connectedness, Mindfulness.

As usual after a long tiresome day, I decided to sip a coffee at Cherries & Berries. Parking the car at the parking slot I walked rather clumsily towards the stairs leading to the shop. When I pushed the glass door, I could smell the brewing of coffees and pastries. Ordering an Espresso, I moved my eyes around the four walls. I could hear the laughter, giggles, loud voices but at the same time they were all distant. Marina, with her cute smile, kept the coffee on the table. I reciprocated back with smile, but i surely knew it lacked any flavour.

I started sipping that delicious frothy drink, unaware of the reality that i was slowly moving into another memory. Memory never dies. It rewinds us to the same moment though sometimes we didn't want to. This time I was taken back to an unplanned journey I had with my husband. The lights, the dinners, the uniqueness of the people, the nature, the ambience; all came to a rush. The camaraderie that i could reinstate was really refreshing, even more refreshing than the coffee i had in my hand.

I am not here to talk about the details of the journey, but it's about the lasting experience that it gave. Have you ever felt that looking at a stunning waterfall or undulating countryside can do more than enrich your social media feed? It unintentionally brought feelings of awe that can bring a number of health benefits. In a 2015 study, researcher Paul Piff of the University of California, Irvine, found that people who spent 60 seconds looking up at towering trees were more likely to report feeling awe, after which they were more likely to help a stranger than people who looked at an equally tall-but far less awe-inspiring-building. "Experiences of awe attune people to things larger than themselves," says Piff. "They cause individuals to feel less entitled, less selfish, and to behave in more generous and helping ways"(Sifferlin, 2016).

There is a strong belief among the indigenous groups that they themselves and nature are part of an extended ecological family that shares ancestry and origins. It is an awareness that life in any environment is viable only when humans view the life surrounding them as kin. Without the human-environmental interface,

life suffers and definitely will lose its sustainability. The modern man is unable to decipher and decode these intentions, but he definitely knows that there is some positive vibe that this environmental canvas provides.

There are two ways to happiness: Hedonic and Eudemonic. In Fourth Century B.C., the Greek philosopher, Aristippus, taught that the ultimate goal in life should be to maximize pleasure and minimising pain, which he referred to as Hedonic happiness. Hedonic happiness is most likely to occur when one engages in fleeting pleasures. While Aristotle, another Greek Philosopher of Fourth Century B.C., first proposed it in his work, Nicomachean Ethics that to achieve happiness, one should live their life in accordance with their virtues. He claimed people are constantly striving to meet their potential and be their best selves, which leads to greater purpose and meaning. Maslow's hierarchy of needs, actually championed a eudemonic perspective on human happiness and flourishing. This kind of enjoyment can improve mood but this is only temporary. While taking a vacation, both these types happen, but for the majority it is hedonic.

Taking pleasure trips outside an individual's usual environment, is seen as an integral feature of human life as they are seen as a mentally and physically healthy pursuit to follow in our leisure time. It has been found that taking vacations can contribute to subjective well-being because people have more opportunities to detach from their work environment, to experience new things, and to control what they want to do during vacations.

In short, travel influences one's overall personal domain. Mathematically as happiness and connectedness are directly proportional to mental health, we can assess that travel definitely imparts direct and indirect effects on overall life satisfaction. In other words a positive and happy mental state can help us to be with our best possible versions, which ultimately guide us to our goals. Achieving accessible and personally meaningful goals is hence associated with subjective wellbeing.

Often the daily mundane routines of life brings a burn out feel. It can lead to depletion of internal resources, which psychologists points out as stress. Travels are really stress relievers. It teaches us the great idea that we have to live in the moment, savour the joy of being with ourselves, with the higher self and with our beings. A healthy mind gives a healthy body too. So for the psychological and physiological wellbeing, small trips are essential.

In a busy schedule where work-life balance is very difficult to maintain, a short stay out, leaves a short-term positive effect within. Though the happiness it leaves is momentary, that beautiful memory itself gives us the strength to move ahead.

Taking vacations helps one stay active and live a healthy lifestyle. It acts as a medicine for stress, depression and mental fatigue. To move, to breathe, to fly, to float, to gain all while you give, to roam the roads of lands remote, to travel is to live: this is what Hans Christian Anderson opined in his book, "The Fairy Tale of My Life": An Autobiography (1847).

Choosing a place brings out colourfully the personality of the traveller. The perspectives as well as his inclinations are well reflected when one chooses the site to enjoy. The moment one selects the destination till the trip is not complete it presents him with invigorating experience. It helps us feel like our best self because we are more willing to receive the world's many lessons, no matter their shape or size. It helps us recognize our shared humanity with others and dissipates fear or misunderstandings. After all, it's much more fun to love the world than to be afraid of it.

To pen down these random thoughts was so refreshing. More than factual detailing of events, recapitulating the time spent together in a short stay made me feel complete. Through the memory of time travel, I was relaxing myself on the soft cushiony sofa of that coffee shop. I had relieved those moments through the compendium of detailed observations. I could say that the coffee that I sipped was Awesome, but more so the memory was ecstatic.

Keeping the notepad aside, I once again grabbed my coffee, but it has become too cold. I smiled and had it as COLD COFFEE. Still I enjoyed my short trip (mini vacation of down the memory lane or in simple back to that past happy moment) to Cherries & Berries.

REFERENCE:

➤ Henderson, Luke Wayne, Tess Knight, and Ben Richardson. "An Exploration of the Well-Being benefits of Hedonic and Eudaimonic Behaviour." *The Journal of Positive Psychology*, vol. 8, no. 4, 2013, pp. 322-336. https://doi.org/10.1080/17439760.2013.803596